PREPARE TO

God's Truth for These Turbulent Days

Grace Turpin

www.shiloah.co.uk
info@shiloah.co.uk

Cover design by Peter Wilks

ISBN 978-0-9523323-4-3

I dedicate this book to all believers in the Lord Jesus and to those who will come to believe in Him.

Contents

BACKGROUND TO THE BOOK

Following in the footsteps of both her father and sister, Frank and Joy Paine, Grace developed a real love for the Word of God – and in particular an understanding of the numbers, the time periods and the calendars that are so deeply embedded in the Bible, especially in relation to the timing and meaning of all the Feasts of Israel.

Once her five children had flown the nest, she sought the Lord for a future calling – desiring to help the Jews in Israel. One morning, the Lord appeared in her room and said, "Will you go to Israel to comfort My hurting people?" So she spent over nine years in Israel, mostly in Jerusalem.

First, she helped an Orthodox family, including helping to care for their son who had survived being blown up by a suicide bomber in the High Street. Later she befriended and comforted lone, English-speaking, Jewish believers, assisting them to settle in Israel. This gave her an amazing opportunity to understand the Bible from a Jewish perspective.

More recently it has been on her heart to see the whole Body of Christ separate themselves unto the Lord Jesus – searching the Scriptures for truth, and to come into unity and expectation of the Rapture of the Church.

She has also studied the various ascensions in the Bible from the point of view of the fulfilment of the Feasts, and now endeavours to encourage the members of the Bride of Christ to be prepared to meet their Bridegroom.

ACKNOWLEDGEMENTS

Firstly I would like to thank our wonderful Lord Jesus Christ for His love and His Holy Spirit, and His faithfulness in teaching me from God my Father's holy precious Word.

I wish to express my sincere appreciation to Oliver Bayley who helped me to get set up at the start and who has supported and encouraged me every step of these three years. Without him it may not have been finished. He compiled the manuscript from the various chapters I had written, followed by Ben Leney who also helped with this as I wrote further chapters and who produced the Index for me.

A special thanks to those who have proof-read chapters, correcting my wording and punctuation, with which I have struggled. These include Sarah, Molly Hawkins, Tony Leney and Martin French.

Thank you to all who have prayed and, in particular, thanks to my youngest daughter, Abigail Usher, for giving the book its up-to-date title and to Peter Wilks for designing the cover. And finally, thanks to Keith Cline for preparing it for publication.

Grace Turpin
11 November 2024

FOREWORD

I suspect that this book has been long in the writing.

Grace's father, Frank Paine, wrote a timely and powerful chronology of the Bible (published in 1994) called 'Miracle of Time – The Day is Almost Over', so Grace was obviously well-schooled in Biblical prophecy and its fulfilment – from which she brings her deep understanding and Biblical exegesis to this book.

It is written in an easy-to-read way and will educate and challenge in equal measure. I have enjoyed reading it and learning from it.

I am pleased to recommend this to every Christian in these Last Days.

Andrew Baguley
Preacher, Teacher & Author

INTRODUCTION

In this book I am hoping to share the truths concerning the End Times in which we are living; showing the order of the events to come, especially concerning the ascension of the Church. We will look at all the ascensions in the Bible and the vital significance of the Jewish Feasts in Leviticus 23; their meaning and their **fulfilment**, past and present, or future.

I also want to share what the Lord has revealed of certain more difficult Bible passages on these matters which have tended to be controversial. We will compare Scripture with Scripture. This is the time for us to be those (Bereans) who search for the Truth which has been hidden in a mystery down the Ages (Acts 17:10-12). The Holy Spirit tells us through Solomon in Proverbs 25:2, 'It is the glory of God to conceal a thing; but the glory of kings is to search out a matter'. Jesus 'has made us kings and priests to His God and Father' (Revelation 1:6) and so it is our honour to search the Scriptures diligently. (The establishment of Israel in the Land started the 'End Times clock' ticking).

The Coming of the Lord Jesus for His Church

Jesus' coming is much nearer than we imagine. Are we waiting in expectancy for this event?

Why I feel constrained in my heart to write to the body of believers about the return of our Bridegroom for His Bride is because lately I have been greatly saddened to find that some dear brothers and sisters have changed their minds on the imminent return of Christ, and are believing that He will come **after** the start of the seven-year Tribulation, which is yet to come.

The greatest sign of His coming is the return of the Jews to their land of Israel and the great restoration of their land and their people in the years since 1948 to this present time. (Besides this there are many signs in Scripture for this 21st Century to consider later as we go on.)

If the Jews had known their Scriptures they would have been expecting their Messiah when He came; for instance, in Daniel 9:22-25 the Angel Gabriel informed Daniel of the timing of Messiah's visitation. They could also have been watching, (as was Simeon in Luke 2:26-32), and if they had heard the prophecy by Zacharias the priest (Luke 1:76-77). Later Jesus expressed His deep sadness over Jerusalem, because they did not know the time of their visitation. See Luke 19:41-44.

Jesus said in Luke 21:8, "Take heed that you not be deceived". There are many voices in circulation as the Bible warns there would be as we see the time approaching. For instance, there are false prophets; there are those who say, 'God has finished with Israel' and so 'the Church will bring in the Kingdom', and, 'the Church must go through the Tribulation', just to name a few. But what does the Bible say?

I was seven years old when I first started reading the Bible and began to enjoy God's Word. My father had an understanding of 'Time' through the Scriptures. God has revealed many Truths. The Bible speaks for itself and answers its own queries, and proves itself to be 100% accurate throughout in the original Hebrew and Greek. By comparing Scripture with Scripture the whole puzzle becomes clearer. Jesus tells us, "For there is nothing covered that will not be revealed, and hidden that will not be known" (Matthew 10:26b). He also said, in John 8:32, "... you shall know the Truth and the Truth shall make you free". Half a truth is **not** truth. I do believe that 'all Scripture is given by inspiration of God', from Genesis 1:1 to the end of Revelation, as Paul says in 2 Timothy 3:16. Also, 'the Word of God lives and abides forever' (1 Peter 1:23).

Christ loved the Church for which He gave Himself – that He might present it to Himself a glorious Church not having spot or wrinkle, or any such thing, but that it should be Holy and without blemish (see Ephesians 5:25 and 27). Therefore in the following pages we shall search the Scriptures together to clarify when in God's Timetable the Rapture could be expected to take place. This is not fixing a date – **NO** – but it is making clear the order of events at this end of the Age.

'Watch, Therefore'

The world needs to be warned of coming Judgement; this is up to each one of us. Isaiah 61:2 says '... to proclaim the acceptable year of the Lord, and the day of vengeance of our God'. Also the Church needs to wake up to the imminence of His return. Romans 13:11 alerts us 'to awake out of sleep; for now our salvation is nearer than when we first believed'. God wants us to know 'truth' that has been hidden in a mystery down these Ages. Daniel was told that the words of his book were closed up and sealed till the time of the end (Daniel 12:9-10).

For 2,000 years the Church has watched and waited in expectancy for Jesus to come, but her members have 'slept' in Christ. Should we not be filled with joy as we see the day approaching? Many may feel He has delayed His return as the word says in Matthew 24:48. This again is a deception, and v.42 says, "Watch therefore, for you do not know what hour your Lord is coming", and in v.44, "... be ready, for the Son of Man is coming at an hour when you do not expect Him."

The devil has blinded many eyes by focusing their gaze upon Scriptures that say that you shall not know what day or hour our Lord shall come, such as in Matthew 25:13 or Mark 13:35-37. We are encouraged to watch and not be ignorant. Of course it will be a different 'moment' for all around the earth!

Matthew 13:39 says '... the harvest is the end of the age' – literally 'the Consummation of the Age'. 'The word 'consummation' in Greek – '*sunteleia*' – does not denote a termination, but the heading up of events to the appointed climax,' Expository Dictionary[1]. Also see Matthew 13:40 & 49; 24:3 and 28:20. This climax will be the start of the final one thousand year period, when Christ comes to reign over the whole world. (Isaiah 9:7 and Luke 1:33. Also see Daniel 9.)

Where are we up to? Firstly, where are we now? We are clearly nearing the end of 2,000 years since Jesus died, arose from death and ascended into heaven, with the promise of His return. We are at the close of this time called 'the Consummation of the Age of the Grace of God'.

So prayerfully come with me through the following pages to find the treasures hidden in God's Holy Word.

[1] 'Expository Dictionary of New Testament Words' by W. E. Vine

CHAPTER ONE

The Ascension of Enoch

There are five ascensions mentioned in the Bible – Enoch, Elijah and Jesus, and two are foretold as still to come.

The word 'rapture' means snatching away, or, carrying away. It is not used in the Bible[1] but it is used by the Church to express the phrases, 'taken (up)', 'carried up', 'ascended', 'translated' and 'caught up' into heaven.

Enoch was the first man to be raptured. We can see him as a picture of the Rapture of the Church, still future. Hebrews 11:5, '**By faith** Enoch was translated so that he should not see death, and was not found, because God had translated him: for before his translation he had this testimony, that he pleased God.' *(AV)* And v.6 says 'without **faith** it is impossible to please ... God.'

Genesis 5:21-24, 'Enoch lived 65 years and begot Methuselah' who was the longest-living man on earth. Enoch had other children and was 365 years old when God took him – i.e. up into heaven – therefore he 'ascended', was 'raptured', was 'taken up' – all describing the same process.

Jude 14-15, 'Enoch, the seventh from Adam' walked with God in a corrupt age (Genesis 6:5). He prophesied before his rapture concerning the second coming of Christ and of Judgement upon the wicked, which will be just before the Millennium. (Noah must have had Enoch's book on board the Ark as he lived before the flood!). Enoch was found to be the subject in apocryphal literature during the Hellenistic period of Judaism. There are many manuscripts of Enoch in Hebrew, Aramaic and Ethiopic – some were found at Qumran[2]. They tell of the Nephilim (giants) of Genesis ch.6. The Holy Spirit caused Jude to include Enoch's prophecy in the Canon of Scripture.

The letters in Hebrew and in Greek each have a numerical value and also a spiritual meaning. Number **7** is God's perfect number, spiritual perfection; it corresponds to the seventh day – the day of rest (Genesis 2:3) and it also pictures the Millennium – when Christ shall come to reign as King of all kings over the whole earth (Revelation 20:1-7). Then there will be peace on earth. In 2 Peter 3:8 he says 'But, beloved, do not forget this one thing, that with the Lord one day is as a thousand years, and a thousand years as one day.' We know there were four thousand years to Jesus' death at Calvary and we are now at the end of two thousand years since then; so the Millennium will be the seventh thousand years of man. Enoch lived 365 years – representing the number of days in a solar year. (The Solar Calendar, as we know it, came into being through Julius Caesar in 45 BC.)

The Bible only records one other man who walked with God and that was Noah; 'Noah was a just man and perfect in his generations. Noah walked with God' (Genesis 6:9). Enoch and Noah are both in the genealogy of Jesus (Luke 3:36-37). Are we walking with God and loving one another? (2 John: 4-6.)

How can we please God? 1 Thessalonians 4:3-4 says, 'For this is the will of God, your sanctification ... that each of you should know how to possess his own vessel in sanctification and honour,' and so be ready for Jesus' return.

Turning to Deuteronomy 33:2-3 Moses also prophesied '... He came with ten thousands of saints; from His right hand came a fiery law for them. Yes, He loves the people; all His saints are in Your hand; they sit down at Your feet; everyone receives Your words.'

Read Revelation 19:11-16 about the second coming of Christ, where v.14 says 'And the armies in heaven, clothed in fine linen, white and clean, followed Him on white horses.' Daniel saw 'in the night visions ... One like the Son of Man, coming with the clouds of heaven! ... Then to Him was given dominion and glory and a kingdom, that all peoples, nations, and languages should serve Him ... ' (Daniel 7:13-14).

Jesus prophesies in answering the High Priest at His trial, "... I say to you, hereafter you will see the Son of Man sitting at the right hand of the Power, and coming on the clouds of heaven" (Matthew 26:64 and Mark 14:62), and Zechariah 14:5b says 'Thus the Lord my God will come, and all the saints with You'.

The prophecy of Enoch in Jude 14-15 says 'Behold, the Lord comes with ten thousands of His saints, to execute judgement on all ...'. This happens at the second coming of the Lord Jesus, at the end of the seven-year Tribulation when He returns with His Church to set up His kingdom on earth. 'Behold, He is coming with clouds, and every eye will see Him, and they also who pierced Him. And all the tribes of the earth will mourn because of Him' (Revelation 1:7).

The wickedness in the earth is becoming so evil that our righteous Holy God has to judge the world. Paul says to Timothy, 'I charge you therefore before God and the Lord Jesus Christ, who will judge the living and the dead at His appearing and His kingdom ...' (2 Timothy 4:1).

So Enoch prophesied, before he was raptured, of the return of the Lord to reign on the earth 'with ten thousands of His saints' (Jude 14).

[1] This word is only to be found in the Vulgate translation, in Latin, where the word *'rapiemur'* meaning 'we will be caught up' or 'we will be taken away' is used. This is from the Latin verb *'rapio'* meaning 'to catch up', hence the English transliteration 'rapture' is now used.

[2] Qumran: copies of the book of Enoch in fragments found at Qumran, near the Dead Sea. See 'Bible Facts' by Ken Johnson.

CHAPTER TWO

The Ascension of Elijah

We come across Elijah the Tishbite, from Gilead, for the first time in 1 Kings 17:1. As is so often the case in God's Word, the meanings of the Hebrew words are significant.

'Elijah' means 'the Lord Jehovah' and 'He is God'. 'Tishbite' means a 'sojourner', that is a 'pilgrim', a 'passer-through', and 'Gilead' means 'a heap of testimony'.

In looking at the Hebrew of these names we can see that Elijah represents in a 'type', or 'picture,' of the Church at her ascension to come. He is also a picture of our own walk with God. As believers in Jesus we have responded to God's gracious call to follow the Lord as our God, and so we too are sojourners in this world and we each have a testimony. Like Elijah, our physical age is not relevant nor is our family background. We are born again of the Spirit of God and await the return of Christ our Bridegroom which He promised, "If I go and prepare a place for you, I will come again and receive you to Myself; that where I am, there you may be also" (John 14:3).

Elijah was the prophet to the northern kingdom of Israel, whose King Ahab married Jezebel, the daughter of Ethbaal, king of the Sidonians. They introduced Israel, and also Judah, to the worship of Baal and killed many prophets of God. It was an extremely dark time in Israel's history. (See from 1 Kings 16:29 onwards.)

Please now read the Ascension of Elijah which is found in 2 Kings 2:1-18.

Elisha, his successor (1 Kings 19:21b), went with Elijah from Gilgal to Bethel, to Jericho and on to the River Jordan. All these places are significant because of the events that had taken place there. At Gilgal, the Children of Israel were circumcised after they entered the Promised Land (Joshua 5:7-9). We have circumcised hearts when we turn away from our worldly ways. (See Deuteronomy 30:6 and Colossians 2:11-15.)

Bethel was where Jacob had dreamed of a ladder on earth reaching up to heaven with angels ascending and descending on it, and the Lord stood above it. There, the Lord had spoken to Jacob and confirmed to him the Abrahamic Covenant (see Genesis 28:12-19). Jericho is the scene of the great battle in Joshua ch.6, so clearly a place signified by manifestations of God's power and by the triumphs of the faith of Israel (Hebrews 11:30-31). Regarding the Jordan River in Joshua ch.3, the Holy Spirit records the crossing of the Jordan by the Children of Israel dry shod. Jordan is also the place of death in baptism (Colossians 2:12).

Elijah, in bidding farewell to the world, visited 'the schools of the prophets' on his way to heaven (2 Kings 2:3). He leaves with them the legacy of his love and counsel. Bishop Christopher Wordsworth[1], helpfully explains that these 'sons of the prophets', or 'schools of the prophets', were established by Elijah. They were teachers of the people in place of the priests and Levites who had been driven from the kingdom of Israel by Jeroboam's idolatry, (see 1 Kings 12:31). Those at Bethel and Jericho knew that Elijah would be taken away from Elisha that day and so too did Elisha, and they might be witnesses of the wonderful event that was about to take place. This would give a clear proof of a future life for which men could prepare themselves.

The translation, or ascension, of Elijah would give them a foretaste, 'in type'[2], of Christ's ascension and the opening of the kingdom of heaven to all believers. Elijah and Elisha crossed the Jordan on dry ground and then, as they talked, suddenly a chariot of fire and horses of fire parted them and Elijah went up by a whirlwind into heaven and Elisha saw it. He picked up the mantle that fell from Elijah and re-crossed the Jordan on dry ground. But the sons of the prophets from Jericho came to meet Elisha and offered to send 50 strong men to search the mountains and valleys in case Elijah had been cast down there. Elisha resisted until in exasperation he said, "Go", but when they returned not having found him, Elisha said to them, "did I not say to you, not to go?"(2 Kings 2:8-18).

Can we see here a type[2] of when the Church is translated, seeing Elijah as the translated Church and Elisha as a type of believing Israel? There are many Gentile believers who love and work in Israel as well as many Messianic Jews who live there. After the Rapture there will be many Jews looking for people they know who have suddenly disappeared and who now cannot be found. It will be very noticeable that they have gone (see Revelation 7:3-4). Maybe, Elisha represents those one hundred and forty four thousand sealed ones who will evangelise the world during the first half of the Tribulation.

We will come across Elijah again in further chapters, but we have seen from what we have covered about him so far that Elijah is a key figure in God's dealings with Israel and the Church.

---

[1] Bishop Christopher Wordsworth, Bishop of Lincoln in the 1880s

[2] 'Types', or 'typology', are where a person, a symbol or an event, usually from the Old Testament, is seen as an example of (or a predecessor to) a future person, concept or event, which is then described, is seen to be fulfilled or which comes to a significant conclusion, normally in the New Testament.

CHAPTER THREE

The Law and the Prophets – Moses and Elijah

'Remember the Law of Moses, My servant, which I commanded him in Horeb for all Israel, ... Behold, I will send you Elijah, the prophet before the coming of the great and dreadful day of the LORD. And He will turn the hearts of the fathers to the children and the hearts of the children to their fathers ...' (Malachi 4:4-6).

Since Malachi penned these words, there has been expectancy by Jews right down to the present day for Elijah to come and fulfil this Scripture, as we shall see.

We will look at the Law and the Prophets in the New Testament, which of course includes Moses, and also compare the similarity of the two prophets.

Then we shall examine the Transfiguration where Moses and Elijah appear with the Lord Jesus in Glory, and then pick up their connection with Revelation ch.11.

Having spent ten years in Jerusalem, I was privileged to attend the Feasts and traditional events in both Orthodox and Christian homes and to experience the Jewish way of life today. It has been the hope of the Jewish people that

Elijah would come at Passover to introduce the Messiah to Israel.

At the Passover Feast an empty chair and a glass is reserved for the Prophet Elijah. When the cup of Elijah is poured a child goes to the door to see if the Prophet is there. Part of a song they sing goes, 'May he come quickly in our day with the Messiah, the Son of David'.

In Matthew 17:10-11 the disciples ask Jesus, "Why then do the scribes say that Elijah must come first?" Jesus confirmed this teaching by saying "Elijah truly is coming first and will restore all things". But before Jesus' first coming, John the Baptist came 'in the spirit and power of Elijah ... to make ready a people prepared for the Lord' (Luke 1:17). This explains why the Jews wondered if John was Elijah (see John 1:19-21). When Jesus asked His disciples, "Who do men say that I, the Son of Man, am?" They answered that some thought He was Elijah... (Matthew 16:13-14). Herod wanted to see Jesus because he had heard that possibly Elijah had appeared, (See Luke 9:7-9). On the tree[1] Jesus cried out loudly "Eloi Eloi ..." and some who heard Him said, "Look, He is calling for Elijah!" and they waited to see if Elijah would come to take Him down (Mark 15:34-36).

In the Sermon on the Mount, Jesus confirms that He is come to fulfil the Law and the Prophets, (Matthew 5:17-18). He summarises Old Testament righteousness in these words, "Therefore, whatever you want men to do to you, do also to them, for this is the Law and the Prophets" (Matthew 7:12, also confirmed in 22:37-40). In John 1:45, Philip says to Nathaniel, "We have found Him of whom Moses in the law, and also the prophets, wrote ... ." Paul, in his defence before Agrippa, states that he, Agrippa, believed the Prophets (Acts 26:27). Paul himself declared "I stand, witnessing both to small and great, saying no other things than those which the prophets and Moses said would come" (Acts 26:22). Many Jews came to Paul in Rome where 'he explained and solemnly testified of the kingdom of God, persuading them concerning Jesus from both the Law of Moses and the Prophets' (Acts 28:23).

The Law is always ascribed to Moses in the Pentateuch, the first five books of the Old Testament. These books present a true and logical introduction to the whole Bible and, in type, comprise a whole summary of divine revelation. I say this to point out that Moses encapsulates the Law, as Elijah does the Prophets.

It is also very interesting to notice the amazing similarities between Moses and Elijah; for example:

- Moses was on Mount Sinai, which is Horeb (Exodus 34:4). Elijah went to Mount Horeb, the Mount of God (1 Kings 19:8).
- Both fasted 40 days.
- Both met with God on Mount Horeb, i.e. Sinai in Arabia. (Galatians 4:24-25). Moses was given the Law by God (Exodus 20), and Elijah was given instructions by God to anoint two kings and a prophet (1 Kings 19:15-16).
- Moses requested for God to take his life, and Elijah requested for himself to die.
- Both were sent to rebuke kings (Pharaoh, Ahab).

- Both took revenge against idolatry.
- Both quenched the thirst of Israel.
- Both divided the waters.
- Both were forewarned of their departure.
- Both are fetched away on the east side of Jordan. Elijah was translated (2 Kings 2) and the body of Moses was buried by God (Deuteronomy 34:5-6). In Jude 9, 'Michael, the archangel, contended with the devil when he disputed about the body of Moses.'
- Both Moses and Elijah conversed with Jesus on the mount of Transfiguration.

So we see from the examples mentioned so far just how closely linked Moses and Elijah are in God's gracious plans for mankind, and for His Covenant people, the Jews in particular. But we are not finished yet!

[1] Peter calls the 'cross' a 'tree' in 2 Peter 2:24.

CHAPTER FOUR

The Transfiguration

We are now going to look at the Transfiguration, because Moses and Elijah are seen with Jesus on the Mount. Then we will explore where in Scripture there is the mention again of 'two men who stood by them' and see if they are the two witnesses of Revelation ch.11.

We shall start in 2 Peter 1:16-18, 'We ... were eyewitnesses of His majesty. For He received from God the Father honour and glory when such a voice came to Him from the Excellent Glory: "This is My beloved Son, in whom I am well pleased." And we heard this voice which came from heaven when we were with Him on the holy mountain.'

This is a mountain scene and therefore a picture, in miniature, of the Kingdom in the Millennium with the Lord in glory; as may be compared with other Mounts such as Moriah, Sinai, Horeb or Carmel, etc., where the mountain top is the scene of a significant encounter between God and the individual(s). A study of 'types'[1] in the Bible will reveal that we can see a glorified Moses typifies the redeemed who have passed through death into the kingdom, and that a glorified Elijah typifies the redeemed who have entered the kingdom by translation into heaven.

It would be helpful now to read Matthew 17:1-9, Mark 9:2-10 and Luke 9:27-36. Matthew and Mark tell us that Jesus led Peter, James and John up into 'a high mountain apart' and Luke adds the words 'to pray'. This mountain is likely to be Mount Hermon, the highest mountain in Israel, about 40 miles north of the Sea of Galilee, for we know from Matthew 16:13 that Jesus and His disciples had recently been close to Caesarea Philippi which is only a few miles away from Mount Hermon.

Now we will concentrate on Luke's account (9:28-36). We read that the disciples 'were heavy with sleep' (v.32) and they awoke to see Jesus transfigured before them. 'His face shone like the sun' (Matthew 17:2), 'and His robe became white and glistening. Then behold, **two men** talked with Him, who were Moses and Elijah, who appeared in glory' (Luke 9:29-31). (We have already established that Moses and Elijah represent the law and the prophets in Chapter 3.)

Now we have to ask the question, "What were they discussing?" They were discussing Jesus' decease *(Greek = 'exodus')* which He was about to accomplish at Jerusalem'.

Why? This must have been significant. Verse 32 says, 'they saw His glory and the **two men who stood with Him**', and then in v.33 Peter names them as Moses and Elijah.

Do we find these two men again in Scripture?

Please now read Luke 23:55 to 24:8. On resurrection morning the women who came from Galilee came to the tomb with spices and found the stone rolled away. 'They were greatly perplexed' and 'behold, **two men stood by them** in shining garments' who told them that Jesus had risen, and that they should 'remember how He spoke to you when He was still in Galilee'. So these **two 'men'** (who would appear to be Moses and Elijah) had witnessed Jesus' resurrection and they rehearsed what Jesus had told them in Galilee. Jesus says to His disciples, "you are witnesses of these things"(Luke 24:48) and so they were, but they all died before AD 100 and could therefore not be 'His witnesses' in Revelation 11:3.

The ascension of Jesus is recorded in Acts 1:9-11. **'Two men stood by them** in white apparel who also said, "Men of Galilee, why do you stand gazing up into heaven? This same Jesus, who is taken up from you into heaven, will so come in like manner as you saw Him go into heaven."'

So if these **two men**, Moses and Elijah, were at the tomb and also at Jesus' ascension, they surely were witnesses to Jesus' death, resurrection and ascension.

We are seeing the great significance that the Lord God has already given to Moses and Elijah, but He is not finished with them just yet! For in Revelation 11:1-12 we learn that, as 'My two witnesses', they will return in the Tribulation[2] to witness to the Jews in Jerusalem. We read, 'when they shall have finished their testimony' (v.7). A dictionary definition for the word 'testimony' being 'evidence stating the true fact'. In other words, they will have testified to the Jews in Jerusalem that they were present at the death, resurrection and ascension of their Messiah.

They will prophesy for 1,260 days in sackcloth. In v.4 'These are the two olive trees and the two lampstands standing before the God of the earth.' This is a quote from Zechariah 4:11-14. 'These are the two anointed ones, who stand beside the Lord of the whole earth.' The next verses of Revelation 11:5-6 tell of what the two witnesses are capable of doing through the power of the Holy Spirit.

References to Elijah are of 'fire', (2 Kings 1:10-12), and 'drought', (1 Kings 17:1 and James 5:17-18). Also references to Moses in Exodus chs.7-11 speak of 'power over waters to turn them to blood and to strike the earth with all plagues as often as they desire'.

So we have seen that Moses was with Elijah on the Mount of Transfiguration with Jesus, discussing His decease which He was about to accomplish at Jerusalem. Luke speaks three times of **two men who stood by them** (Luke 9:32, 24:4 and in Acts 1:10). They were witnesses of Jesus' death, resurrection and ascension. Why? Because they are, as Jesus calls them in Revelation 11:3, '**My two witnesses**' who return to Jerusalem at the start of the Tribulation[2] to witness to the Jews about their Messiah of Isaiah 53 and many other Scriptures. Hallelujah!

From all these interesting incidents and references, I believe we can see the importance of these **two men** in God's plan of redemption, regarding His chosen people the Jews. Oh that their eyes are opened to behold their Messiah – who was, and is and is to come!

[1] See note on 'Types' at end of Chapter 2, on page 16.

[2] The Tribulation, which is yet to come, will commence with the antichrist confirming the covenant with the Jews for seven years (Daniel 9:27), and the 1,260 days mentioned above refers to the first half of the seven years of the Tribulation, a period which is also called 'a time, times and half a time' of 360-day (Babylonian) years. The second half of the Tribulation is measured in 'times' but also as '42 months' because Jesus says in Matthew 24:22 and Mark 13:20 'unless those days were shortened, no flesh would be saved' at the end of the Tribulation (Revelation 11:2 & 13:5).

CHAPTER FIVE

The Ascension of the Lord's Two Witnesses

To set the scene for this chapter, we need to understand that a 'third Temple' will be built by the Jews in Jerusalem at the start of the Tribulation[1]. It won't take long to build, as almost everything is already made and prepared, including the furnishings and the priestly garments. Interestingly, a red heifer of three years old (and without any white hairs) will be needed for the sanctification of the priests (Numbers 19:2). Examples have now been reared and, in due time, when we have gone at the Rapture and this third Temple has been built, they'll be used for this purpose.

Read Revelation 11:1-13 about the two witnesses. John is told to 'measure the temple of God, the altar and those who worship there' (vv.1-2). If we look back to Lamentations 2:8-9 we see that 'He has stretched out a measuring line' and this for destruction; 'The Law is no more, and her prophets find no vision from the LORD.' So what it is saying is that John is to measure the spiritual state of the people who will be worshipping there. But the outer court of the temple, which has been given to the Gentiles, will be trodden under foot for forty-two months – the latter half of the Tribulation.

Next, the angel tells John, "I will give power to **My two witnesses** and they shall prophesy for 1,260 days clothed in sackcloth." As you will remember from my previous chapter, 1,260 days refers to the first half of the Tribulation. These two witnesses are Moses and Elijah, 'the two anointed ones, who stand beside the Lord of the whole earth' (Zechariah 4:14). In Matthew 17:11 Jesus said, 'Elijah truly is coming first and will restore all things'. Elijah and Moses will tell the Jews that Jesus truly is their Messiah, who died at Calvary and rose again from death the third day and that He ascended up to heaven forty days later. Also that He will return to set up His Kingdom on earth; and, that they are His witnesses because they were there watching all these events take place.

They have come to tell them, as the Scriptures have promised in Malachi 4:4-6. During those days Moses and Elijah will prophesy and work many signs and miracles. Their testimony will be known worldwide; 'peoples, tribes, tongues, and nations' will have been tormented as a result of their ministry (see Revelation 11:5-6, 9-10).

When the two witnesses have finished their testimony at the mid-point of the Tribulation, when the animal sacrifices are ended by the beast[2], the beast will kill them. Their dead bodies will lie in the streets of Jerusalem for three and a half days for all to **see**, and no-one will be allowed to bury their bodies. The peoples of the world, who can **watch** what is happening by TV, smartphone and tablet, will celebrate and rejoice and even send gifts to one another, because they will no longer be tormented by these two prophets. "After the three and a half days, the breath of life from God" enters them and they stand up raised to life, so that all who **see** them will be filled with great fear. Next, a great voice from heaven sounds, saying, "Come up here," (see also Revelation 4:1) and they ascend up to heaven in a cloud and their enemies will **see** them go.

Now this is amazing! When Jesus was taken down from the tree, He was put in a tomb, a stone was rolled across the entrance, and when He arose from the dead, only the two witnesses, Moses and Elijah, and believers **saw** Him alive. Then, when He ascended into heaven, only the two witnesses and the eleven disciples **saw** Him go. However when these witnesses die, they lie out in the open for all to **see**. When they arise to life and hear the voice to ascend up to heaven, it will be the Jews and unbelievers who **observe** it and hear the voice (Revelation 11:7-12).

Jesus said to Thomas, "Because you have **seen** Me, you have believed. Blessed are those who have not seen and yet have believed" (John 20:29). Can you imagine the response there will be to this very public event?

This truly is a demonstration of God's LOVE and GRACE for His Jewish people! The two witnesses have been preaching to the Jews for over three years to persuade them that Jesus is their Messiah, and finally there is an enactment through Moses and Elijah of death, resurrection and ascension which the Jews hopefully, cannot deny. (See Luke 16:31).

'For God so loved the world, that He gave His only begotten Son, that whosoever believes in Him should not perish but have everlasting life' (John 3:16).

Here God is demonstrating His LOVE through His two witnesses. All they have reported from having been present at the death, resurrection and ascension of Jesus has only to be believed, for He truly was and is the promised Messiah to Israel.

God has never stopped loving His Jewish people whom He chose. Through Abraham, Isaac and Jacob and his descendants, He gave the Law and the Prophets, and finally His only beloved Son to be their Messiah. There has always been a remnant of believing Jews, but God wants the whole nation to believe in Him. During these past 2,000 years God has been preparing a Bride for His Son; but during the coming seven years of tribulation He will restore the Jewish people to worship Him alone. Those who endure to the end will all believe in Him (see Romans 11:26).

Read Hosea 2:14-23 to feel the heart of God for Israel – **God's mercy on His people**. "Therefore, behold, I will allure her, will bring her into the wilderness and speak comfort to her. I will give her her vineyards from there, and the Valley of Achor as a door of hope; she shall sing there, as in the days of her youth, as in the day when she came up from the land of Egypt. "And it shall be in that day," says the LORD, "That you will call Me 'My Husband,' and no longer call Me 'My Master,'... (v.18) In that day I shall make a covenant with them ... to make them lie down safely (v.19). I will betroth you to Me forever; Yes, I will betroth you to Me in righteousness and justice, in loving kindness and mercy; I will betroth you to Me in faithfulness, and you shall know the LORD ... (v.23b). Then I will say to those who were not My people,

'You are My people!' And they shall say, 'You are my God!'"

'Oh, the depth of the riches both of the wisdom and knowledge of God, how unsearchable are His judgements and His ways past finding out!' (Romans 11:33).

[1] The Tribulation. See end of previous Chapter for explanation.

[2] The Beast. See Revelation ch.13 and Daniel 9:27b.

CHAPTER SIX

The Fulfilment of The Feasts of The LORD

Leviticus 23 is a very important chapter in the Scriptures as it gives all the feasts of the LORD. These feasts are of course Jewish feasts, so, because Jesus Himself observed them faithfully, they have great relevance for believers in deepening our understanding of why Jesus spoke and acted as He did. 'Speak to the children of Israel, and say to them: "The feasts of the LORD, which you shall proclaim to be holy convocations, these are **MY feasts**"' (v.2). These were joyful, holy gatherings.

Israel's year was divided by seven great feasts and furnishes us with a perfect view of God's dealings with Israel throughout their history. Actually it is HIS STORY foretold through these feasts, as we are about to find out through looking at their spiritual meaning.

Jesus came to fulfil all the law (see Matthew 5:17-18) and that fulfilling is based on the framework provided by the feasts.

A Chart showing the timings of the Feasts is shown as Appendix 1 on page 119.

The Sabbath

The Sabbath is also a feast of the LORD, a day of rest to enjoy Him. 'Six days shall work be done, but the seventh day is a Sabbath of solemn rest, a holy convocation. You shall do no work on it; it is the Sabbath of the LORD in all your dwellings' (Leviticus 23:3). The Sabbath occupies a unique and independent place; from creation through to its great fulfilment in the seventh thousand years of rest (i.e. the Millennium); when Satan is bound, and the Lord Jesus comes to reign upon this earth as King of kings and Lord of lords for a thousand years (see Revelation 17:14, 19:16 and 20:1-4; also compare Zechariah 14:9).

This will be the Kingdom for which millions have prayed; when the Church of God has awakened to the reality that the great 6 days (that is 6,000 years) are at an end, and the Kingdom is about to come and transform this planet from being a shambles into a scene of blessing and enlightenment for the whole human race[1].

The Seven Feasts

Returning to the seven feasts of Leviticus 23, they are the Feast of Passover, the Feast of Unleavened Bread, the Feast of Firstfruits, the Feast of Weeks, the Feast of Trumpets, the Day of Atonement, and the Feast of Tabernacles.

We will look at these separately to see if we can determine which ones Jesus has fulfilled, is fulfilling now, or is yet to fulfil. Generally they were feasts of great thanksgiving and praise; only the Day of Atonement was a day to recap on one's life, and repent, and adjust, and humble oneself.

The Feast of Passover

Read Exodus 12:1-14 where we are given a detailed account of how this feast was to be kept yearly in remembrance of how God delivered the children of Israel out of slavery in Egypt. 'On the fourteenth day of the first month' (Abib, or Nisan, it was full moon) 'at twilight is the LORD's Passover' (Leviticus 23:5). On whatever day of the week it was, they were to take an innocent lamb of the first year without blemish, on the tenth day, and keep it four days before they were to kill it. They were then to sprinkle the blood of the lamb on the lintel and doorposts of their homes. "For when" the LORD "sees the blood" on the doors He "will pass over the door and not allow the destroyer to come into your houses to strike you"(Exodus 12:23).

So the Passover established in a very graphic manner the vital principle, granted by the LORD, of repentant sinners being protected from His divine judgment by their sheltering under the blood of an innocent lamb slain on their behalf. Today, Israel keeps the Passover yearly but without a temple, so there are no sacrifices of biblical animals; they use chickens instead. Sadly they eat the unleavened bread without understanding the true meaning of it. God saw each Passover lamb as looking forward to the sacrifice of His beloved Son '**the Lamb of God**' who would take away the sin of the world (see John 1:29). Jesus was holy and without blemish; no sin was found in Him (2 Corinthians 5:21 and 1 Peter 2:22). Jesus laid down His life for us (1 John 3:16).

Jesus, proclaiming His ministry, read in the synagogue from Isaiah 61:1-2a, 'The Spirit of the Lord GOD is upon Me, because the LORD has anointed Me to preach good tidings to the poor; He has sent Me to heal the broken-hearted, to proclaim liberty to the captives, and the opening of the prison to those who are bound; to proclaim the acceptable year of the LORD' (see also Luke 4:18-19). 'He taught' the people 'as one having authority' (Matthew 7:29). 'He cast out the spirits with a word, and healed all who were sick' (8:16b). 'He was moved with compassion' toward the multitudes, and healed them (14:14) and He taught them (Mark 6:34b).

On the evening before His death, Jesus took the Passover with His disciples. This occasion is known today by various names, such as the Lord's Supper, 'breaking of bread' (even though that term and the Lord's Supper clearly were different occasions in the days of the Early Church), 'Holy Communion', the 'Eucharist' or the 'Mass'. The word 'Easter', (falling each year close to the Passover date and marking the death and resurrection of the Lord Jesus as the Lamb of God) is unfortunately of pagan origin. At this 'Last Supper' Jesus introduced all believers in Him to a **New** Covenant in His sinless blood, (Matthew 26:28, Mark 14:24), and in verse 19 of Luke 22 He said, "Do **this** in remembrance of **Me**." The Holy Spirit through Paul added in, 1 Corinthians 11:26, 'till He comes'.

This was the New Covenant to take the place of the Passover, which remembered the Jews' deliverance out of Egypt. Now, it is the Passover for all believers in Christ; for us to look back in remembrance to Jesus' crucifixion at Calvary, and understand that Jesus has 'passed all those who believe in Him, over from eternal death to eternal life, having shed His blood to forgive us all our sin. The Church has done this for 1,990+ years so far and will continue to do so until Jesus comes again. 'For indeed Christ, our Passover was sacrificed for us' (1 Corinthians 5:7b). Also, when Jesus took the bread and the cup, He was in essence saying, 'Here is the Priesthood of Melchizedek restored to Me' (see Genesis 14:18–20; Psalm 110:4 and Hebrews 5:5–10). 'For we do not have a High Priest who cannot sympathise with our weaknesses, but was in all points tempted as we are, yet without sin' (Hebrews 4:15).

The sufferings of the Lord Jesus are described in all four Gospels including His experience in the garden of Gethsemane where His sweat was as great drops of blood, as He anticipated, despite having no sin in Himself, that He was to take the sin of the whole world upon His body on the tree (Luke 22:39-46). Isaiah 53 expresses the suffering Jesus was to bear, 'He was led as a lamb to the slaughter' (v.7). His back was ripped raw from the stripes He bore to take away our sicknesses. 'His visage was marred more than any man, and His form more than the sons of men' (Isaiah 52:14). Psalm 22:1-18 also prophetically describes His sufferings.

GOD raised Jesus from death because it was not possible that He should be held by death (Acts 2:24). So the Feast of Passover was fulfilled when our Lord Jesus, the true Lamb of God, hung on that tree and died, shedding His sinless, innocent blood on our behalf. That shedding means the **LORD GOD**, in His righteous judgment, 'passed over' all those who have claimed by faith the protection of Jesus' blood, for themselves; Jesus being the true and ultimate 'Lamb of God', as was said earlier; and in another sense, that shedding allows all who believe in Jesus' sacrifice (which comes from two words meaning 'given and holy') to pass from death unto LIFE, that is ETERNAL LIFE (John 17:2-3 and Romans 6:23).

So can you see how Jesus fulfilled the Feast of Passover for us?

In later Chapters the fulfilment of the other six remaining Feasts of Leviticus will be explained.

[1] To understand God's great time pattern through the Bible see 'Miracle of Time' by Frank L. Paine, which may be downloaded free from www.shiloah.co.uk/miracle-of-time.
Charts within Frank's book are a great help to our understanding of God's sovereign use of time over and within His creation.

CHAPTER SEVEN

The Feast of Unleavened Bread

Jesus said to the twelve disciples "There is nothing covered that will not be revealed, and hidden that will not be known" (Matthew 10:26).

Clarence Larkin[1] defines this Feast like this: 'As the Passover is a type of the death of Christ, so the Feast of Unleavened Bread is a type of the 'Walk' of the Believer, and there should be no interval between salvation of a soul and its entrance on a holy life and walk. The 'seven days' point to the whole course of the Believer's walk after conversion. The typical teaching then of the Feast of Unleavened Bread is that, having been saved by the shed blood of Christ our Passover, we are to 'walk' in newness of life, purging out the leaven of worldliness, and doing no 'servile work', or 'work that is done to earn salvation'.

We will be looking at the spiritual meaning of unleavened bread and leaven, as well as looking at Scriptures of the taking of unleavened bread and what they picture. Then we will look at how the children of Israel fulfilled this feast at the Exodus out of Egypt; before seeing how Jesus fulfils this Feast for our Exodus. (See Chart of 'The Seven Days of Unleavened Bread' – Appendix 2, page 120.)

The Spiritual Meaning of Unleavened Bread

Unleavened bread is baked without any raising agent added, i.e. yeast. Let us look at the meal, or grain offering, in Leviticus 2:1-4. We know that the fine flour of this offering here, when it was in the grain form, was unleavened anyway, but when made into flour here, it had to remain unleavened, because the yeast, that is, the 'leaven', represents sin. So this meal offering so wonderfully represents the life of Jesus as seen by the Father in all His perfection. There is no blood in the meal offering because it is in relation to the life of Jesus. Jesus was without the 'leaven' of sin, 'For' God 'made Him who knew no sin to be sin for us ...' (2 Corinthians 5:21), and so in His Father's sight Jesus was – and is – indeed the pure unleavened bread. The whole sixth chapter of John is about bread, first the natural and then the spiritual. Five times Jesus refers to Himself as the 'bread of Life' and in v.33 He says "For the bread of God is He who comes down from heaven and gives life to the world," and that bread from heaven is unleavened – it is pure and sinless.

Paul says, 'let us keep the feast, not with old leaven, nor with the leaven of malice and wickedness, but with the unleavened bread of sincerity and truth' (1 Corinthians 5:8). In the Spirit we feed on the living Word of God. The Word is Truth. 'In the beginning was the Word and the Word was with God and the Word was God' and continually exists. 'In Him was life and the life was the light of men' (John 1:1 & 4). Light dispels darkness, and truth reveals error. 'God has given us eternal life, and this life is in His Son. He who has the Son has life; he who does not have the Son of God does not have life' (1 John 5:11-12).

Jesus says "I am the way, the truth and the life" (John 14:6). In the disciples' prayer which we pray so regularly we say, 'Give us this day our daily bread'. Yes, this can mean food, but also to feast in the Word of God daily. 'The words of the LORD are pure words, like silver tried in a furnace of earth, purified seven times' (Psalm 12:6). 'All Scripture is given by inspiration of God', or God breathed, 'and is profitable for doctrine, for reproof, for correction, for instruction in righteousness' (2 Timothy 3:16). The Word is unleavened bread.

In Deuteronomy 16:3, unleavened bread is referred to as 'bread of affliction'. Why do you think that is so? Could it be that truth is not always palliative? (See 1 John 1:8-10.)

So What is Leaven?

Leaven is pride, it puffs up, is something added. Read 1 Corinthians 5:6-8, 'a little leaven leavens the whole lump', and in verse 8 we get 'the leaven of malice and wickedness'. Jesus said, "Take heed and beware of the leaven of the Pharisees and the Sadducees" (Matthew 16:6), explained in verse 12 as their 'doctrine', or teachings, and which in Luke 12:1 He calls, 'hypocrisy'. Leaven speaks of truth mixed with the doctrines and the thoughts of man. In reality it is a corruption of the Word of God – man's own interpretation without the witness of the Holy Spirit. Much has become religious tradition in the Church down the centuries to our present day. Sadly, when truths have been revealed there have often been breakaways from a church with a new sect starting – often resulting in many differing sects. Yet, Jesus prayed to the Father, "I do not pray for these alone, but also for those who will believe in

Me through their word; that they all may be one, as You, Father, are in Me, and I in You; that they also may be one in Us, that the world may believe that You sent Me" (John 17:20-21).

Lot is seen eating unleavened bread before he leaves Sodom (Genesis 19:3). Can you see here a picture of the Church feeding on the Truth of the Word of God before her rapture out of this world, just before judgement falls on the Earth?

There is another picture in 1 Samuel 28:24-25 where Saul eats unleavened bread before the battle in which he dies.

Feast of Unleavened Bread Kept at The Exodus

Leviticus 23:5-8

'On the fourteenth day of the first month at twilight is the LORD's Passover. And on the fifteenth day of the same month is the Feast of Unleavened Bread to the LORD; seven days you must eat unleavened bread. On the first day you shall have a holy convocation; you shall do no customary work on it,' and the same on the seventh day.

Here I would like to give a further explanation of the number 7 (also see my previous Chapter 1). The meaning of the number 7 is spiritual perfection and it occurs throughout the Bible. There are 7 days of creation, 7 days in a week, 7 days to a Jewish wedding. The number 7 often infers the Church, or Bride of Christ, which covers 2,000 years since her birth at Calvary to the Rapture of the Church. Later we will look at the leavening of the Church which happens and is seen prophetically in the 7 churches of Revelation.

These seven days are a picture looking back to their deliverance out of Egypt and forward to Christ in His Church.

The Feast of Unleavened Bread was acted out by the children of Israel at the Exodus in obedience to God's instructions through Moses. (See Exodus 12:15-20 and 13:3-10 for the seven-day journey from Egypt.) 'The people took their dough before it was leavened, having their kneading bowls bound up in their clothes on their shoulders' (Exodus 12:34). In verse 39 'they baked unleavened cakes of the dough which they brought out of Egypt, for it was not leavened, because they were driven out of Egypt and could not wait, nor had they prepared provisions for themselves'. They were to 'keep this ordinance in its season from year to year' (Exodus 13:10).

Numbers 33:1-9 describes the **seven days** of unleavened bread following the Passover as the children of Israel came out of Egypt.

Day 1 They journeyed from Rameses in Egypt and camped that night at Succoth.

Day 2 They journeyed from Succoth and camped in Etham at the edge of the wilderness.

Day 3 They turned south and travelled down through the mountains by a large wadi to Pi Hahiroth between Migdol and the sea, called today Nuweiba on the Gulf of Aqaba, and in the morning crossed the Red Sea (See evidence of this in a book called 'The Exodus Case', by Lennart Moller[2]).

Days 4, 5, and 6 They travelled through the wilderness of Etham to Marah where the people were thirsty, and there the bitter waters were healed. All the time they ate unleavened bread.

So they came to Elim on **Day 7** where there were twelve wells of water, and seventy palm trees. (Both 'seventy' and 'palm trees' are always associated with the Gentiles in Scripture, just as the number twelve is with Israel); and they camped there by the waters. Elim is a beautiful picture of the coming Kingdom of Christ where the Gentile world; originally seventy nations (see Genesis ch.10), will be blessed by Israel (see Genesis 22:18).

Because people query how all the children of Israel, a possible two million people, could have travelled so far in those first three days, I find it important to share the following explanation. I do believe the Scriptures explain this. First of all they were fleeing from Pharaoh, not just having an afternoon stroll! Moses, as we know, was brought up by Pharaohs' daughter as a son. In Acts 7:22 we are told that 'Moses was learned in all the wisdom of the Egyptians and was mighty in words and deeds'. He was 40 years old when he fled from Egypt and dwelt in Midian, east of the Red Sea. He was 80 when he returned to Egypt with his brother, Aaron, to deliver his people from there to bring them firstly, back to the mountain of God in Midian as God had said (see Exodus 3:12). Pharaoh drove them out of his land (Exodus 6:1). The obvious route that Moses knew was to aim straight for the north of the Gulf of Aqabah and then turn south to Mount Horeb, the mountain of God; today it is called Jabel al-Lawz, ('mountain of the law').

So they 'journeyed from Rameses,' after eating the LORD's Passover, 'about six hundred thousand men on foot besides children,'...'and a great deal of livestock' ... 'all the armies of the LORD' (Exodus 12:37and 41). 'God led the people ... and (they) went up in orderly ranks out of the land of Egypt' (Exodus 13:18). Four times in this chapter it says that 'by strength of hand the LORD brought them out of Egypt'. 'They went out with boldness in the sight of all the Egyptians'... 'and they camped at Succoth' (Numbers 33:3 and 5). 'And the LORD went before them by day in a pillar of cloud to lead the way, and by night in a pillar of fire to give them light, so as to go by day and night. He did not take away the pillar of cloud by day, or the pillar of fire by night from before the people' (Exodus 13:21-22). The moon, though on the wane, would not have been bright enough for them to travel through desert or wilderness darkness. The song of Moses says 'You in Your mercy have led forth the people whom You have redeemed; You have guided them in Your strength to Your holy habitation' (Exodus 15:13).

So I hope that you can see that with God in charge and plenty of men to help the families and flocks along, they could travel for many hours not curtailed by darkness or weary children as they could also ride on their donkeys!

How Jesus Fulfils The Feast of Unleavened Bread in His Own Life

Remember these feasts are called by the Lord, 'My feasts' in Leviticus 23:2. Later we will look at the Scriptures concerning Jesus' resurrection and ascension, but here we will start from the evening of the Last Supper, or Passover meal, which He spent with his disciples; the day beginning at 6 pm (Thursday) to 6 pm (Friday which was the start of the Jews' Passover). They ate unleavened bread at the Passover meal and for the following seven days. This, as we have seen represents feasting on the Word of God in sincerity and truth which Jesus shared with them. And He was Himself the unleavened bread.

Judas having left the room, Jesus shared with the eleven disciples those great chapters of John 14–16, closing with His own wonderful prayer to His Father in John 17. After this they left the city and went down to the Garden of Gethsemane.

In the Garden of Gethsemane Jesus came victoriously through the toughest temptation in His life on earth, as He travailed in prayer with His Father. He was to face the coming experiences of the trial and sufferings, knowing what it would cost 'when His soul was made an offering for sin' (Isaiah 53:10). That was one thing; but worst of all, was to know that His Father, God, would forsake Him when He bore the sin of the world upon Himself on the tree, would be agony indeed (Matthew 27:46). What brought Jesus from heaven to die at Calvary was the Fall – that great primal sin of independence from God our creator. Crucifixion was the only way (John 12:31-33) and Jesus only wanted God's Will to be done – there was no other way. There in the garden Jesus was arrested and taken to the High Priest's house to be tried.

Under Jewish law and judgement by the high priests, scribes and elders Jesus stood composed and silent, except under oath when He had to answer. He was charged with blasphemy (see Matthew 26:63-65). Blasphemy had to include the name 'God' but Jesus spoke calling Himself "the Son of Man" not 'God' so he did not blaspheme, even as far as the 'law' was concerned. The Jews condemned Jesus, their Messiah, to the death of crucifixion; and in so doing they broke twenty-one laws in sentencing their Messiah to death.

Next morning the chief priests and elders took Jesus before Pilate who after talking with Him could find no fault in Him. Pilate then sent Him to Herod; there Jesus, the King of kings, stood silent before an immoral king who, with his men, mocked Him and returned Him to Pilate. The Jews had worked up such a frenzy by this time causing a tumult, and telling Pilate that he was no friend of Caesar's, until Pilate gave into their wishes (Matthew 27:24-26). After having Jesus scourged he delivered Him to the cruel, Roman soldiers who mocked Him and plaited a thorny crown on His head which they beat down on His head before leading Him away to be crucified between two criminals, at the time of the morning sacrifice; Jesus was that Lamb of God.

Jesus, having His hands and feet nailed to the stake could only speak. He prayed forgiveness for His Gentile, Roman persecutors. He spoke compassion with love for His mother, and salvation for the penitent thief – Forgiveness, Love and Salvation.

Jesus was crucified between 8 am and 9 am. Darkness covered the land from noon until 3 pm, after which Jesus cried out to His Father, then He shouted "It is finished" and said, "Father, into Your hands I commend My spirit." He bowed His head and 'breathed His last' (Luke 23:46).

His body was buried before 6 pm. Jesus, the LAMB of GOD, had become our Passover Lamb to pass all who believe in Him, over from death to eternal Life. Glory to God!

Throughout, Jesus our Saviour fulfilled the prophesies concerning the Messiah in the Bible.

Note God does not count time to one who is dead, as we don't; so from this fact it is as if the day when Jesus died was followed immediately by Jesus' resurrection as if those days and nights in death did not occur. This is amazingly expressed in one long sentence in Matthew 27: 51-53, where the time interval that occurred, halfway through verse 51, between Jesus' death and His resurrection, is completely ignored by the Holy Spirit writing through Matthew, *from this aspect only*. This means also that Jesus rose from death on the first *day* of the **weeks** to Pentecost (not 'week' as interpreted in all our Bibles). The Hebrew is *'sabbaton'* which is plural – see Deuteronomy 16:16 and Exodus 34:22, **the Feast of Weeks).**[3]

Read Luke 24:1-48 where Jesus appeared to two disciples on the way to Emmaus. Notice in verses 27 and 44 the repetition of "all things must be fulfilled, which were written in the Law of Moses and the Prophets and in the Psalms concerning Me", and verse 45 'And He opened their understanding, that they might comprehend the Scriptures.' It was that night (Thomas being absent), when Jesus appeared to the ten disciples gathered in the room in Jerusalem where 'He breathed on them and said to them, "Receive the Holy Spirit"' (see John 20:19-22).

There are no records of any sightings of Jesus through the rest of this week of unleavened bread. It mentions in John 20:26-29 the 'eighth day' when Thomas saw the Lord and believed; but Jesus says, "Blessed are those who have not seen and yet have believed". I think this has a prophetic implication to be understood as we look at how the Church is seen not to keep the feast of unleavened bread down these 2,000 years.

So can you see here that the whole of redemption's story, from the night of His Passover meal with His disciples and His resurrection when he revealed Himself alive to those on the way to Emmaus and expounded to them in all the Scriptures; and again that night in Jerusalem when He shared the things concerning Himself from many Old Testament passages. This was Jesus fulfilling the Feast of Unleavened Bread. It was seven days from God's view-point and our redemption was completed within that time.

Later we shall look at Revelation chapters 3 and 4 showing the leaven that has entered the Church in its seven phases of Church history to the present day.

[1] 'Dispensational Truth' by Clarence Larkin – page 159

[2] 'The Exodus Case' by Lennart Moller

[3] The Feast of Weeks – see Chapter 9

CHAPTER EIGHT

The Resurrection of Jesus and His Fulfilment of The Feast of Firstfruits

It is necessary to look first at the resurrection of the Lord Jesus and the immediate events that took place on that morning.

In Matthew 27:50-53 we read, 'The veil of the temple was torn in two from top to bottom' (see also Hebrews 10:20). 'The earth quaked and the rocks were split, and the graves were opened; and many bodies of the saints who had fallen asleep' *(died)* 'were raised; and coming out of the graves after Jesus' resurrection, they went into the holy city and appeared to many.'

Who do we think these saints were? They could have included people like Simeon, Anna the widow, Zacharias and Elisabeth, Joseph (Jesus' step-father – presumed to have died), the penitent thief and others who had believed on Jesus as their Messiah during His life and ministry. These resurrected saints and Jesus constituted the sheaf of Firstfruits which was waved to the Lord that morning[1]. 'The first of the firstfruits of your land you shall bring into the house of the LORD your God' (Exodus 23:19). In John 12:24, referring to His death, Jesus said 'unless a grain of wheat falls into the ground and dies, it remains alone; but if it dies, it produces much grain'. Jesus has cleansed us from sin by His death and consequential resurrection; so that we, as His Church, can enter heaven.

The Feast of Firstfruits

Leviticus 23:9-17

Jesus was fulfilling the Feast of Firstfruits when He rose from the dead. This feast was all to do with the beginning of the harvest when the first stalks were picked and gathered into a sheaf to be waved before the LORD, to be accepted for the people. No one was to eat bread until after the sheaf had been waved. The harvest itself speaks of the gathering-in of all who believe on the Lord Jesus as their Saviour. As such, it is an expression of the Church of Jesus Christ down these 2,000 years until Jesus comes for His Church, the Bride, at our ascension, see verses 15-17, which describe the second part of the harvest offerings, fifty days later.

Jesus, being our High Priest, was to appear before God to present Himself to His Father. We need to know this now in order to understand what Jesus was saying to Mary Magdalene, and was about to do that morning (see John 20:1-18). Mary Magdalene, finding the stone rolled away from the sepulchre, went to tell Peter and John. They ran to the sepulchre, but seeing that the body was not there returned home. Mary, having returned, stood outside weeping – it was then that Jesus, full of compassion, appeared to her. He calls her name "**Mary!**" She turned, "Rabboni!" she cries. Jesus says, "**Do not touch Me**, ***not yet***" *(correct translation).* Why not? "I have not yet ascended to My Father ... I am ascending to My Father and your Father, and to My God, and your God." What beautiful words!

Later that morning Jesus appeared to several women 'and they came and **held Him** by the feet and worshipped Him' (Matthew 28:9). By this time He had returned from heaven, but how wonderful that Jesus our Bridegroom should appear to this woman, Mary Magdalene, known as a sinner, who had been delivered from **seven** demons (Luke 8:2) and say these words to her "I ascend to My Father and your Father, and to My God and your God." Surely she is a picture of the Bride. Can you see this? We are cleansed and forgiven and Jesus has made a way for us to come into the presence of God the Father through our Saviour's blood, shed at Calvary. (The number '**seven**' is associated with the Church.)

It is worth reading the whole of Hebrews chapter 9. Jesus our risen Saviour, the Son of God, was to appear in heaven before the Father having accomplished the purpose for which He had come to this earth and to present His atoning blood in heaven. 'Christ came as High Priest ... with His own blood He entered the Most Holy Place once for all, having obtained eternal redemption *for us*' (vv.11-12), and 'without shedding of blood there is no remission' (v.22). Christ ... entered ... into heaven itself, now to appear in the presence of God for us;' (v.24) ... 'but now, once ..., He has appeared to put away sin by the sacrifice of

Himself' (v.26). 'For by one offering He has perfected for ever those who are being sanctified' (10:14).

We are aware that this does appear to show that Jesus ascended twice – once on the morning of His resurrection and again forty days later.

Once a year Aaron, as High Priest, took the blood of a bull, as a sin offering inside the veil of the Tabernacle and sprinkled it seven times on the mercy seat to make atonement for himself, his household and for all the congregation of Israel (see Leviticus 16). This was on the Day of Atonement. Therefore we understand here that Jesus, as our High Priest, resurrected, ascended up into heaven to present His own sinless blood, before the Father, on the mercy seat to atone for every believer. Jesus has atoned once and forever for all believers.

The LORD says "I, even I, am He who blots out your transgressions for My own sake, and will not remember your sins" (Isaiah 43:25).

'The life of the flesh is in the blood and I have given it to you upon the altar to make atonement for your souls; for it is the blood that makes atonement for the soul' (Leviticus 17:11).

'Therefore, brethren, having boldness to enter the Holiest by the blood of Jesus, by a new and living way which He consecrated for us, through the veil, that is, His flesh, and having a High Priest over the house of God, let us draw near with a true heart in full assurance of faith, having our hearts sprinkled from an evil conscience and our bodies washed with pure water' (Hebrews 10:19-22).

When God the Father sees the blood of His beloved Son, He looks at us and sees Jesus.

So we see here that at Jesus' resurrection He ascended to His Father in heaven to place His sinless blood on the mercy seat before God our Father, and now we can sing:

I can stand in His presence, clothed in robes of purest white,
I can talk to Him daily at His Throne;
For His blood has made me righteous,
And His love has drawn me near,
And I'm precious to Him, precious, I'm His own.

Liza (Elisabeth) Collins 1979

[1] See 'Miracle of Time' by Frank L. Paine – pages 71-72 *and* 'The Restored Vision' by Arthur E. Ware – pages 418-422.

CHAPTER NINE

The Feast of Weeks *(Part 1)*
The Ascension of Jesus

The Feast of Weeks Leviticus 23:15-22

'You shall count for yourselves from the day after the Sabbath, from the day that you brought the sheaf of the wave offering: seven Sabbaths shall be completed. Count fifty days to the day after the seventh Sabbath; then you shall offer a new grain offering to the LORD. You shall bring from your habitations two wave loaves ... They shall be of fine flour; they shall be baked with leaven' (vv.15-17).

So from the Feast of Firstfruits that we saw in my previous chapter, there was to be seven weeks and then a fiftieth day. In all our Bibles, in connection with the resurrection of Jesus, we have the expression 'the first day of the wee**k**'. See Matthew 28:1; Mark 16:2 & 9; Luke 24:1; John 20:1 & 19 and Acts 20:7. But the Greek *'te mia ton sabbaton'*, correctly translated, is 'the first day of the wee**ks**' or 'sabbath**s**.' *'Mia'* = first, *'sabbaton'* is **plural** and refers to the seven week**s** or Sabbath**s** from the waving of the sheaf of the firstfruits (on the first day) of the harvest to when the bulk of the harvest was to be safely gathered in: 'Count fifty days to the day after the seventh Sabbath' (Leviticus 23:16a).

At this time, in AD 33, Jesus was **partially** fulfilling the Jewish Feast of Weeks. We know that Jesus then ascended on the fortieth day of this Feast and that the disciples had to wait, on their own, for another nine days without Him, so He personally didn't fulfil this part of the Feast at that time. Then, on the Day of Pentecost (the 50th day) the Holy Spirit came upon the waiting disciples, as recorded in Acts 2. (Later we will address these 'missing' nine or ten days – which, as I say, were unfulfilled at that time[1].)

Luke, in writing to Theophilus, tells that Jesus presented 'Himself alive after His suffering by many infallible proofs' and 'speaking of the things pertaining to the kingdom of God', being seen by His believing followers for forty days (Acts 1:3).

What was Jesus accomplishing during the 40 days of those seven weeks to Pentecost?

Firstly it would be good to read Luke 24:13-35. Later on, on the first day of His resurrection, Jesus joined two disciples walking to Emmaus and asked what they were discussing and why they were sad. When they had rehearsed the events of the past day, Jesus spoke, saying that they were "slow of heart to believe in all that the prophets have spoken." He went on, '"Ought not the Christ to have suffered these things and to have entered into His glory?" And beginning at Moses and all the Prophets, He expounded to them in all the Scriptures the things concerning Himself.'

When they arrived at their destination they invited Jesus in to eat with them. At the meal 'He took bread, blessed and broke it and gave it to them. Then their eyes were opened and they knew Him; and He vanished from their sight.' These two disciples returned to Jerusalem, saying "Did not our heart burn within us, while He talked with us" ... and "opened the Scriptures to us?" They joined the ten disciples – Thomas was not present – and shared their story. Also they heard that Jesus had appeared to Peter.

Jesus suddenly appeared in their midst, but they were all terrified! He spoke Peace to them and showed them His hands, feet and side. Then He asked for food to which they gave Him broiled fish and some honeycomb and He ate in front of them.

It was on this occasion that Jesus breathed on them and said, "Receive the Holy Spirit" (John 20:22). We can see that this breathing of the Holy Spirit upon them was also in its way a 'firstfruits', which was followed at Pentecost by the Holy Spirit being fully outpoured on the gathered disciples as seen in Acts 2:1-4.

'He opened their understanding that they might comprehend the Scriptures' about His suffering, death and His resurrection on the third day. He instructed them 'that repentance and remission of sins should be preached in His name to all nations beginning at Jerusalem' (see Luke 24:47).

Eight days later when Thomas was present Jesus again appeared. Thomas believed when he saw the wounds (John 20:24-29). There were many other signs Jesus did in the presence of His disciples which were not written down. Jesus showed Himself to seven of His close disciples at the sea of Tiberius where He gave His eighth 'Sign Miracle' recorded by John: the miracle of the catch of 153 great fishes in a net which did not break. They had breakfast together by the sea and Jesus restored Peter from his denial of Jesus at His trial, then He commissioned him (John 21).

In 1 Corinthians 15:3-7 Paul declares to the Corinthians how he had preached that Christ died for our sins according to the Scriptures and that He rose again the third day according to the Scriptures. Jesus had been seen by Peter and later by more than 500 brethren at one time. Also he appeared to James, His half-brother, who became a pillar in the church in Jerusalem. (Acts 12:17 & 15:13).

Jesus could not have taught these things before He went to Calvary because the disciples were still in disbelief and hoping that He was going to, at that time, restore the Kingdom to Israel (also see Acts 1:6). For many years afterwards the believers would only have the Old Testament of the Bible, so it was imperative that they should understand that Jesus was portrayed throughout their Scriptures. Now that we have the New Testament, it is entirely relevant that we also, Jew and Gentile, study the whole of Scripture.

Finally the Lord commissioned His disciples. Jesus had appointed them to meet Him on a mountain in Galilee. He said, "All authority has been given to Me in heaven and on earth. Go therefore and make disciples of all the nations, baptising them ... , teaching them to observe all things that I have commanded you" (Matthew 28:18-20), and we can add from Mark 16:15-17, to "preach the gospel to every creature. He who believes and is baptised will be saved; ... And these signs will follow those who believe: In My name they will cast out demons; they will speak with new tongues; ... they will lay hands on the sick and they will recover." They were to preach repentance and > *page 58* >

The Fulfilment of The Feast of Weeks

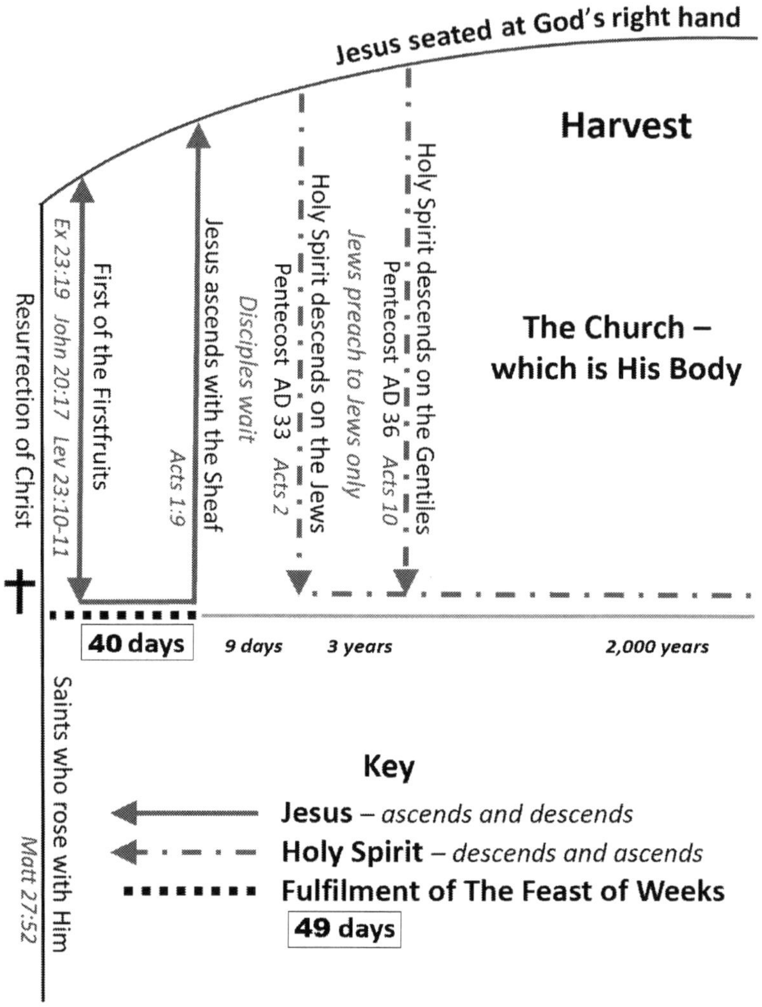

The Feast of Weeks lasted 49 days, or seven weeks, with Pentecost being on the 50th day. From Jesus' Resurrection to His Ascension were only the first 40 days of this Feast of Weeks. There were then nine days of this Feast when Jesus was not on the earth before the Holy Spirit came at Pentecost, the 50th day.

Shown are the three years between the Holy Spirit descending on the Jews of Pentecost in AD 33 and then on the Gentiles in AD 36.

The Fulfilment of The Feast of Weeks

For part 2 see Chapter 19 on page 102.

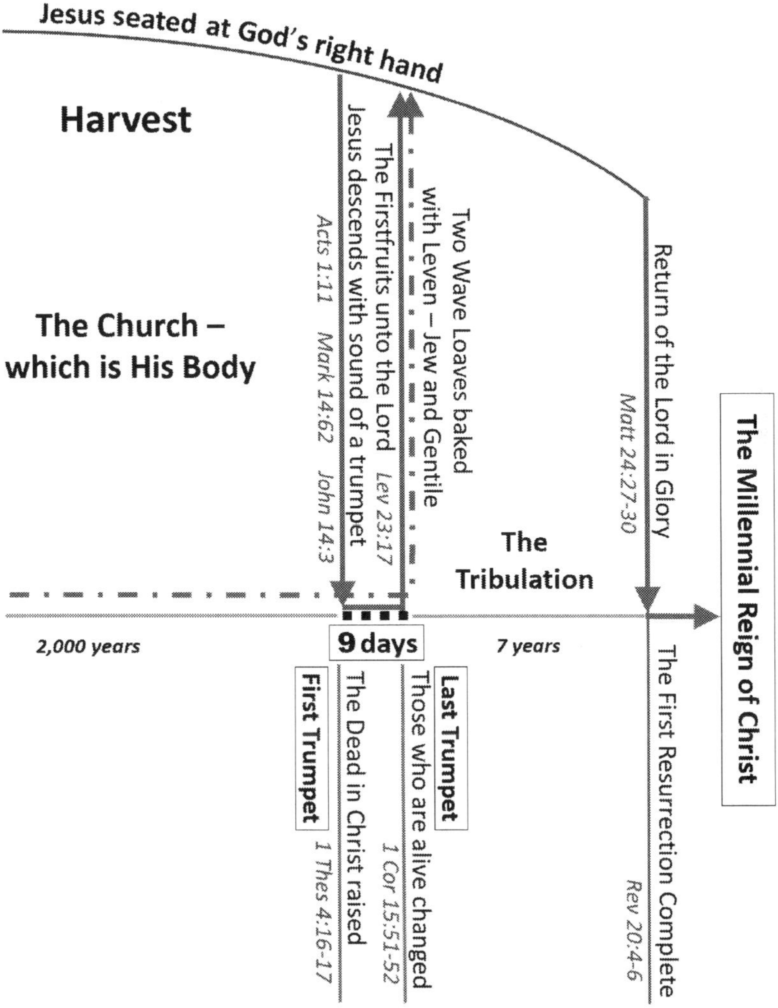

Completion of the Feast of Weeks, Leviticus 23

Jesus is to fulfill the last ten days of the Feast of Weeks when He returns to the earth with the raised 'dead in Christ' when 'the first trump' is sounded from heaven. For nine days He will appear to believers around the earth before we all, as a united Bride, ascend with the Holy Spirit 'to meet the Lord in the air' [1].

There is a complete version of this chart as Appendix 3 on page 121.

> *page 55* > remission of sins in Jesus' Name, beginning at Jerusalem. Jesus said to them, "Behold, I send the Promise of My Father upon you; but tarry in the city of Jerusalem until you are endued with power from on high." So His promise to the disciples was that they should wait for the Holy Spirit to come upon them in Jerusalem (Luke 24:47-49).

We are so blessed to have the living word of God to feed our hungry souls upon, and to build up one another!

The Ascension of Jesus

The Book of Matthew, written primarily to the Jews, does not mention the ascension of the Lord Jesus. In Mark 16:19 it says that Jesus 'was received up to heaven and sat down at the right hand of God'. At the stoning of Stephen, 'he, being full of the Holy Spirit, gazed into heaven and saw the glory of God, and Jesus standing at the right hand of God, and' Stephen 'said, "Look! I see the heavens opened and the Son of Man standing at the right hand of God!"(Acts 7:55-56).

Luke records that Jesus led His disciples out to Bethany, which is on the top of the Mount of Olives, 'and He lifted up His hands and blessed them'. As He did this 'He was parted from them and carried up into heaven. And they worshipped Him' (Luke 24:50-52). From Acts 1:6 it appears that the disciples had just asked Jesus if He was now going to restore the kingdom to Israel, but Jesus explained that they would not need to be concerned about that which was the business of His Father God. However, they would receive the power of the Holy Spirit to witness in Jerusalem, Judea and Samaria and unto the ends of the earth. Then, 'while they watched' Jesus 'was taken up, and a cloud received Him out of their sight'. It was then that 'two men', who we have seen to be Moses and Elijah[2], 'stood by them in white apparel, who also said, "Men of Galilee, why do you stand gazing up into heaven? This same Jesus, who was taken up from you into heaven, will so come in like manner as you saw Him go into heaven" '(Acts 1:9-11).

Hebrews 9:26, "Now ... He has appeared to put away sin by the sacrifice of Himself." Jesus showed Himself alive to many disciples as well as the women who had ministered to Him in Galilee. He opened to them the Scriptures concerning Himself from Moses, the Psalms and the Prophets. Also He bade them to go and make disciples from Jerusalem to the then known world doing what they had seen Jesus do during His ministry. The eleven disciples watched Him ascend into heaven.

These two Feasts, Firstfruits and Weeks, speak of Harvest. As the Passover looked forward to the sacrifice of Jesus, meaning 'Saviour' coming to offer Himself as the Lamb of God, so these feasts look forward to the completed formation of the Bride of Christ, the Church. The seven churches of Revelation 2 and 3 represent the journey the Church has taken through these 2,000 years. The whole Church will be raptured together to the heavenly home that Jesus has prepared for us, so that 'where He is there we shall be also' (John 14:2-3).

For Jesus to fulfil this feast **He needs to be on the earth for another nine days**. Therefore, when we look at the 'Ascension of the Church' we will look at the fulfilment of those final nine days of the Feast of Weeks to Pentecost when the Harvest is fully gathered in (see my Chapter 20)[1].

1 See 'Ten Days At The Rapture' by Brian Gemmell.

2 Moses and Elijah – See my Chapters 3 and 4.

CHAPTER TEN

The Birth and Early Days of The Church

God gave Jesus 'to be head over all things to the church, which is His body, the fullness of Him who fills all in all' (Ephesians 1:22-23).

The Birth of The Church

Only John's Gospel, which is written for the Church, records the following passage: that a soldier pierced the side of the dead body of Jesus and out came blood and water (John 19:31-34). Can you see the birth of the Bride of Christ there? Every baby is born out of blood and water. Eve was formed out of Adam's side while Adam was in a deep sleep (Genesis 2:21-24). Woman was formed from Adam's side and she became his wife. See 1 Corinthians 15:21-23, 45-49.

Another picture of the Church can be seen in the Gospel of John, 20:6-8, after Jesus' resurrection when Peter and John went to the tomb. They 'saw the linen clothes lying there and the handkerchief', or napkin, 'that had been around His head, not lying with the linen clothes, but folded together in a place by itself'. Paul says, 'He is the head of the body, the Church, which is the beginning, the firstborn from the dead, that in all things He may have the pre-eminence.' (Colossians 1:18). Jesus, the head, has risen, but the Church, being the body is not yet raised. As it were, we are still in the grave clothes, not yet ascended. 'The body is sown in corruption, it is raised in incorruption' ... 'It is sown a natural body, it is raised a spiritual body' (1 Corinthians 15:42 & 44). At evening on the day Jesus rose from the dead, 'He breathed on them and said to them, "Receive the Holy Spirit"' (John 20:19-22).

The Early Church

We have just seen the birth of the Church of Jesus Christ out of Jesus' pierced side, and on the day of His resurrection He breathed the Holy Spirit on His disciples. On the Day of Pentecost the Holy Spirit was poured out upon the 120 (Acts 1:15) waiting in the 'house where they were sitting'. They were filled with the Holy Spirit and spoke in tongues 'as the Spirit gave them utterance' (Acts 2:1-4).

The early church fed on 'the unleavened bread of sincerity and truth' (1 Corinthians 5:8). So what was this 'Truth'? Jesus said, 'I am the Way, the Truth and the Life' (John 14:6). It was all that Jesus had shared during His three and a half years of ministry, and in particular, all He said to the disciples the night He was betrayed and in the days following His resurrection before He ascended to heaven.

The early believers only had the Old Testament, so we have to go to the Acts of the Apostles to see how the truths were spread through the believers. Of course, hundreds of people had testimonies of healing, deliverance and, cleansing from leprosy, having all been touched by Jesus

Himself during His few years of ministry. There were also ongoing miracles through the disciples, after they were filled with the Holy Spirit on the day of Pentecost. We have sermons by Peter and Stephen recorded in Acts 2 and 7. 'And they continued steadfastly in the Apostles' doctrine and fellowship, in the breaking of bread, and in prayers' (Acts 2:42). 'So continuing daily with one accord in the temple, and breaking bread from house to house, they ate their food with gladness and simplicity of heart, praising God and having favour with all the people. And the Lord added to the Church daily those who were being saved' (vv.46-47).

As well as those who believed in Jesus during His time of ministry, there were 3,000 saved on the Day of Pentecost (Acts 2:41) and another 5,000 men shortly after that (Acts 4:4).

Later in Acts 4 we read: 'The multitude of those who believed was of one heart and one soul ... they had all things in common. And with great power the apostles gave witness to the resurrection of the Lord Jesus' (v.32-33). 'Believers were increasingly added to the Lord, multitudes of both men and women' (Acts 5:14). 'And daily in the temple, and in every house, they did not cease teaching and preaching Jesus as the Christ' (v.42). 'The word of God spread, and the number of the disciples multiplied greatly in Jerusalem, and a great many of the priests were obedient to the faith' (Acts 6:7).

This was the Church in its unleavened state and it continued to grow through persecution, first from the Jewish leaders and later from the pagans and the Roman

Emperors, as the Church spread out into the then-known world.

Sadly, there was the incident in Acts 5:1-11, where a couple lied about the cost of their possession which they had sold, pretending to have given the whole proceeds to the Church. Their sudden death put the fear of God into the believers. This was leaven smartly dealt with by the Holy Spirit through Peter.

The Church, down these 2,000 years has kept Roman time with pagan names to the days of the week and the months of the year, and has not kept the Jewish feasts. However, this may change in the Millennium, because Jesus will be reigning over the whole earth from Jerusalem with God's earthly people. 'He changes the times and the seasons' (Daniel 2:21).

What a wonderful beginning to the Church of Jesus Christ, the Bride being formed for her Bridegroom!

CHAPTER ELEVEN

How Leaven Has Entered The Church of Jesus Christ

Revelation Chapters 2 and 3

The character of these seven churches described here in Revelation 2 and 3 was their exact condition in John's day when he wrote the Book of 'The Revelation of Jesus Christ', as directed by God the Father, through God the Son, via the angel sent by Jesus to John (see Revelation 1:1-2). But they also give a prophetic view of the programme of the Church down these 2,000 years to the Rapture of the Church.

Daniel 12:4 says, 'But you, Daniel, shut up the words and seal the Book until the time of the end ... .' However, in Revelation 22:10, John is told by the angel not to 'seal the words of the prophecy of **this** book, for the time is at hand'. So we see these two instructions, to seal and then not to seal, allowing for the lapse of time between Daniel and John. This has given rise to the belief by some that the Book of Revelation is only about the actual times of John, and if so, this book is now therefore of little relevance for us today, nearly 2,000 years later. **But** that understanding

cannot be true! It is true that, as we find often with Biblical prophecy, there are multi-fulfilments of prophecy which start small and end with a greater and final fulfilment, rather like the principle of 'types' followed later by their 'antitypes', which would mean that some current events in John's time might have some, though small, place in the Book of Revelation 2,000 years ago. However, what we do know is that chapters 6-19 are prophetic and still future through the Tribulation and into the Millennium.

Not only are the words about these seven churches good descriptions of their present state in John's time, they also indicate particular phases of Church history over the centuries, as well as in our present day in different parts of the world. For instance we can clearly see that the Laodicean Church is typical of our present Western culture today. The thoughts and actions of man have been added to the Truths in the Word of God bringing in traditions and heresies distorting the Truths in Scripture.

Before any disciples of Jesus went to the Gentiles, these seven cities in Turkey had pagans worshipping foreign gods in temples; but Jews also living there had synagogues and worshipped God according to the law, plus all the extra laws which had been added since leaving Babylon.

Now we are going to take a brief walk through Church history from Revelation chapters 2 and 3 which, as well as being churches established by the Apostles at that time, are also prophetic, referring to future seasons down through the 2,000 years to our present day. They show how leaven has polluted the whole Church and how these characteristics are all present somewhere around the world today. I have studied these chapters many times, but it is only recently that God has shown me the relevance of the leaven.

First let us look at a parable that Jesus gave in Matthew 13:33, 'The kingdom of heaven is like unto leaven which a woman took and hid in three measures of meal till the whole was leavened'. In 1 Corinthians 5:6-8, leaven is compared to malice and wickedness. It equates man-made traditions and religion to evil doctrines, and scepticism to the supernatural, being as worldliness. This was explained in my Chapter 7.

It may help now to read Revelation chapters 1-4. In chapters 2 and 3 the Lord reveals to John the gradual 'leavening' of the Church throughout the Church age, right up to our present day, where we see now that the whole Church has become leavened. We need to see how the truth which Jesus taught the disciples, practiced in the Gospels and the Acts and taught in the Epistles, has been leavened through the centuries. The messages to the seven churches are inserted between two visions; the first vision is of Christ in the midst of the seven lampstands, or early churches, in chapter 1, and the vision of the twenty-four elders around the throne in chapter 4. The latter is a vision of the glorified Church, Jew and Gentile with the Lord, after her being caught up to heaven (1 Thessalonians 4:13-17); and so encapsulates chapters 2 and 3 of Revelation. The Church is not seen again until Revelation 19, after the seven year tribulation, and in vv.11-14 Jesus descends from heaven with us as the armies in heaven – following Him on white horses – as He comes to reign on the earth.

The interpretation of the messages to the seven churches has been a mystery down the centuries, causing believers to watch in expectancy for the return of Jesus Christ as He promised.

We shall now look at the characteristics of each church and date it in its prophetic timing in history as we can now see it to be. This whole 2,000 years of the history of the Church is, of course, the Harvest being gathered in.

The disciples of Jesus will sit on thrones – see what Jesus says to His disciples when Peter asked Him "what shall we have?" as Peter had just said, "We have left all and followed You." So Jesus said to them, "Assuredly I say to you, that in the regeneration, when the Son of Man sits on the throne of His glory, you who have followed Me will also sit on twelve thrones, judging the twelve tribes of Israel ... " (Matthew 19:27-28). On the night of Jesus' betrayal He said to His disciples "You are those who have continued with Me in My trials. And I bestow upon you a kingdom, just as My Father bestowed one upon Me, that you may eat and drink at My table in My kingdom, and sit on thrones judging the twelve tribes of Israel" (Luke 22:28-30). Judas will not be among them but maybe Paul will instead? 'The Lord said to Ananias, "Go, for he, (Paul) is a chosen vessel of Mine to bear My name before Gentiles, kings, and the children of Israel ..."' (Acts 9:15-16). And, 'Paul, a servant of Jesus Christ, called to be an apostle, separated to the gospel of God' (Romans 1:1).

This has been an introduction to the seven churches in Revelation and in the following six chapters I explain the leaven which has infiltrated the Church over the last 2,000 years.

CHAPTER TWELVE

The Churches of Ephesus and Smyrna

Ephesus

The Backslidden Church of Revelation 2:1-7

This church represents the time period from AD 70 – 170.

Paul was the first of the Apostles to go to Ephesus in Turkey, as far as we know. He was on his second missionary journey and he left Priscilla and Aquila there (Acts 18:18-19). Apollos, a Jew mighty in the Scriptures, taught at Ephesus though he knew only the baptism of John the Baptist. Aquila and Priscilla took him aside and explained the way of God to him more accurately (Acts 18:24-28). Later Paul taught the word of the Lord there for two years. He had found twelve disciples of John the Baptist and he introduced them to the Holy Spirit. He baptised them 'in the name of the Lord Jesus', laid hands on them and 'the Holy Spirit came upon them and they spoke with tongues and prophesied' (19:5-6). 'God worked unusual miracles by the hands of Paul' and there was a wonderful work of God wrought in Ephesus and 'the word of the Lord grew mightily and prevailed' (Acts 19:11-20).

Ephesus had many temples but the outstanding one was the Great Temple of Artemis to the goddess Diana. The silversmiths traded their wares in her honour. That Temple was considered to be one of the seven wonders of the world.

In Paul's parting message to the elders of the Church of Ephesus when returning from his third missionary journey, he exhorted them. He warned them saying, "For I know this, that after my departure savage wolves will come in among you, not sparing the flock. Also from among yourselves men will rise up, speaking perverse things, to draw away the disciples after themselves. Therefore watch, and remember ..." (Acts 20:29-31).

Paul wrote the Epistle 'to the saints who are in Ephesus and faithful in Christ Jesus' (Ephesians 1:1), in which we see the Love of God manifested. He says 'that Christ may dwell in your hearts through faith; that you, being rooted and grounded in love, may be able to comprehend with all the saints ... and ... to know the love of Christ which passes knowledge; that you may be filled with all the fullness of God' (Ephesians 3:17-19). Paul gave many other words of encouragement and ends his letter, 'Grace be with all those who love our Lord Jesus Christ in sincerity' (Ephesians 6:24).

Paul (with Priscilla and Aquila) was well acquainted with spiritual warfare – hence the chapter on the armour of God (Ephesians 6).

These letters to the seven churches were probably written as circulars to be passed on to the other six churches.

Sadly when John was writing the Book of Revelation the church of Ephesus had 'left their first love' and he warned them to 'repent and do the first works' (Revelation 2:5). They hated the deeds of the Nicolaitans, which God also hated. Here Paul's wolves are called Nicolaitans. *'Niko'* means 'to conquer' and *'laos'* means 'the people' or 'laity'. This was not in accordance with New Testament teaching of shepherd or pastor, thus introducing Clergy, Bishops and Archbishops, etc. The Ephesians recognised some of them to be false apostles. This was the start of leaven entering the Church which has continued throughout the Church Age to our present day.

Smyrna

The Persecuted Church of Revelation 2:8-11

Smyrna has for its root meaning 'bitterness' and means 'myrrh', an ointment associated with death. The description of this church prophetically speaks of persecution followed by death, from AD 170 to Constantine in AD 312. Jesus addresses Himself as the First and the Last, who was dead, and came to life. He says he knows their tribulation, and their suffering and how impoverished they are. He bids them, saying, "Be faithful until death, and I will give you the crown of life," – the martyrs' crown.

These believers at Smyrna were being persecuted firstly by Jews, as Jesus and Stephen were, and then by pagans and Romans. It was a great test of faith and Jesus was telling them not to fear what they were to suffer, that it was the devil behind it. The devil and synagogue of Satan are both named here. Those who overcame did not compromise.

Referring to the prophetical period of time, its duration would be 'ten days'. This could be either the ten great persecutions under the Roman Emperors between Nero and Diocletian – seven of which occurred during the Smyrna period of Church history, or it could refer to the ten years of fierce persecution under Diocletian. Jesus had no rebuke for this church and no request for repentance. There was no added 'leaven' to the church during this period of time.

Today there are countries where Christians are suffering in like manner, such as in Nigeria, Afghanistan and other countries you can probably name. These believers can take comfort in Paul's words in Philippians 3:10 'That I may know Him and the power of His resurrection and the fellowship of His sufferings being conformed to His death.' Be faithful!

CHAPTER THIRTEEN

The Church of Pergamos

The Licentious Church of Revelation 2:12-17

'Pergamos' means 'a towered city', but its hidden meaning is also the fiery marriage of church and state from the Greek words *'pur'* for 'fire' and *'gamos'* for 'marriage'. It was the capital city of this Asian province. It was also the centre of the official religion of Emperor Worship, the deification of the Head of State. It was the first to build a temple to this imperial cult and it also supported four other major pagan cults. Pergamos was Satan's throne in John's day. (When Attalus III, the priest-king of the Chaldean hierarchy, fled there before the conquering Persians, Satan moved his capital from Babylon to Pergamos.) At first Satan persecuted the believers in Jesus, and Antipas was one of the faithful martyrs (2:13). But later Satan changed his tactics and began to exalt the church through Constantine who united the church and state. The altar of Pergamos is now in Berlin. *(Search 'Pergamos' or 'Pergamon' on line).*

'Antipas' means 'dissenter' and stands for any Christian who refused to worship the Emperor as a god. The Lord is seen wielding His sharp two-edged sword of the Word of God (2:12) against the corrupting influence of Balaam and the doctrine of the Nicolaitans whose names in both

Hebrew and Greek mean 'lord of the people' and symbolise authoritarian leadership. Jesus says "Repent, or else I will come to you quickly and will fight against them with the sword of My mouth" (2:16).

Prophetically, Pergamos represented AD 312 – 606 commencing from the accession of Constantine, which saw the church married to the state – which oozed with idolatry. In AD 312 it is told that Constantine had a vision of a cross. This became the sign of Christianity and from it came the state religion of the Roman Empire.

The Council of Nicaea in AD 325 held in Turkey, was the first great meeting of the wider Christian church and it was called by the Emperor Constantine. The church through this council was divided into the Western division, the Papal church based in Rome, and the Eastern Division, the Greek church based in Constantinople. These two Divisions are represented by the legs of the great image that Nebuchadnezzar saw in Daniel chapter 2.

Constantine's decisions have affected the souls of millions who have come after him. The only good he really did was to put an end to the persecutions of his predecessor, Diocletian. Constantine worshipped the sun god in which he trusted for success in war as he was a military Emperor. Christian festivals were amalgamated with pagan festivals such as the birth of Christ, the Son of God, united with the birthday of the pagan sun god to occur on December 25th. The Passover became 'Easter' from 'Ostarte', a northern goddess of spring whose symbol was a rabbit. Jewish feast days were abolished including Shabbat, and Sunday was made the day of worship. The Bible was translated from Hebrew and Greek into Latin.

The Roman Empire collapsed in AD 435 and with it the end of *Pax Romana*[1].

'It was at this time that "Post-Millennial Views" had their origin.' This is a false belief which now deserves our attention. 'As the Church had become rich and powerful, it was suggested that by the union of Church and State a condition of affairs would develop that would usher in the Millennium without the return of Christ, and since some scriptural support was needed for such a doctrine, it was claimed that the Jews had been cast off 'forever', and that all the prophesies of Israel's future glory were intended for the Church' (quote from Clarence Larkin)[2]. This belief has continued in much of Western Christendom to this day which is a complete deception. Check out Romans 9, 10 & 11 and Jeremiah 31, for a start. This doctrine has been believed because of ignorance of Scripture and false teaching in the theological colleges.

However, today against all possible human odds, the Jews are back in the land of Israel that God gave to them and were declared a nation in 1948 on time. Scripturally – some years ago the Spirit of God revealed the significance of the number of days between Simeon's great prophecy of Luke 2:34 to do with the 'rising of many in Israel' and the fulfilment of his words in 1948 (see Miracle of Time)[3]. 'Who has seen such a thing? Shall the earth be made to bring forth in one day? Or shall a nation be born at once ...?' (Isaiah 66:8). True, they have mainly come back in unbelief, but by the end of the Tribulation to come, those who survive will all believe in their MESSIAH. 'Blindness *(or hardening)* in part has happened to Israel until the fullness of the Gentiles has come in. And so all Israel will be saved.' 'They are beloved for the sake of the fathers' (Romans 11: 25-26 and 28).

There is one more 'until passage' in Luke 21:24 where Jesus tells us, 'And Jerusalem will be trampled by Gentiles until the times of the Gentiles are fulfilled.' Jerusalem has belonged once more to the Jews and to the State of Israel – a vital pointer to Jesus' prophecy being fulfilled, when God set His seal upon Israel's repossession of her land and holy city at the close of the Six Day War in 1967 (Miracle of Time)[4]. While there is still the small matter of two mosques existing on the Temple Mount, we simply watch this space with expectation.

So from these Scriptural examples, among many others, we know three certainties:

1) That the Lord has **NOT** finished with the Jews;

2) That therefore the Old Testament promises of blessing for the Jews apply to the Jews! – and **NOT** to the Church;

3) That the Post-Millennial view for the return of Christ, after the church has supposedly built His Kingdom for Him all by herself, is **a dangerous, misleading lie**.

Praise God! So the Scriptural prophetic sequence of future events and future periods of time fits best as follows:

Event 1, the Rapture, the removal of the true Church (1 Thessalonians 4:13-18); followed by the seven-year Tribulation (e.g. Daniel 9:27); followed by:

Event 2, the visible return of Christ in glory at the end of the Tribulation (e.g. Matthew 24:29-31); which is followed by the Millennial reign of Christ on earth (e.g. Revelation 20:1-6).

In summing up, the Lord's words to the churches of Smyrna and Pergamos apply directly to us Christians today. Persecution and suffering will come for Jews and Christians, as 'the spiritual war in high places' (from Ephesians 6:12), grows ever fiercer towards the end. Our reaction is to be the same as those who have trodden this path before us: we stand firm; we fear not; we stay faithful; we repent of sins when necessary; we rejoice, and again we rejoice; and we remain assured of the great truth that in Christ, He has promised, "Lo, I am with you always, even unto the end of the Age" (Matthew 28:20).

'But thanks be to God, who gives us the victory through our Lord Jesus Christ' (1 Corinthians 15:57).

[1] *'Pax Romana'* – an approximately 200-year period of Roman history: a golden age of Roman imperialism, relative peace *('pax')*, prosperity and stability.

[2] 'The Book of Revelation' by Clarence Larkin – page 23

[3] 'Miracle of Time' by Frank L. Paine – page 137

[4] 'Miracle of Time' by Frank L. Paine – page 185

CHAPTER FOURTEEN

The Church of Thyatira

The Corrupt Church of Revelation 2:18-29

The name of Thyatira comes from the root word 'to sacrifice'. In John's day this city was an important manufacturing centre, producing prized purple garments in the indigo trade made from the roots of plants, and also pottery and brass. It was a stronghold of occult trade societies, or guilds, given to pagan worship of Madonna, Astarte and immorality. Tradesmen were obligated to be members.

Paul and Silas stayed in Philippi with a woman called Lydia, a seller of purple, from Thyatira (Acts 16:14).

The true believers were commended for their works, love, faith, patience and service; but in the church they were tolerating a dominant female, probably rich and influential, who was given the name of Jezebel as she was so like the wife of Ahab (see 1 Kings 16:31 and 18:13). As a type, she speaks of the corruption of true Christianity by false religion, which was introduced by the Catholic Church and is 'Mystery Babylon' of Revelation 17, which is still future. Jezebel called herself a prophetess, and the Christian saints of Thyatira allowed her to teach destructive doctrines to seduce the members to commit fornication and to eat things sacrificed to idols. God gave her space to repent of her fornication but she did not (Revelation 2:21).

Prophetically this church extended from AD 606 when Boniface 3rd, the first Pope, was crowned Universal Bishop, to AD 1520. These were the dark Middle Ages with the crusades and the inquisition. This 'Thyatiran Age' went through three stages:

1) From Boniface 3rd to Gregory 7th – The **growth** of the Papacy.

2) From Gregory 7th to Boniface 7th – The **full sway** of the Papacy.

3) From Boniface 7th to The Reformation – The **declining** of the Papacy.

This Thyatiran Age lasted nearly a thousand years, from the fall of the Roman Empire to Luther's '95 Theses', and we can clearly see the Lord's patience through it all!

This church was riddled with greed and corruption, immorality, idolatry and heresy. Satan's secret societies sprang up everywhere including Freemasonry, the Templars and Jesuits – wielding power from within; and purple-robed prelates attacked any manifestation of the true Christian faith – as for example in their treatment of the Lollards, John Wycliffe and Jan Hus. Those leaving the state church might lose their jobs, but God would meet their need with spiritual manna and life in the Spirit.

Some leaven entered the church during this time, for example:

AD 709 – Kissing the Pope's feet. This came from Emperor worship.

AD 995 – Canonization of dead saints, started by Pope John 15th.

AD 998 – The tradition of fasting on Fridays and during Lent was introduced.

AD 1050 – The Mass was first declared to be the sacrifice of Christ.

AD 1079 – Celibacy of priests and nuns. (All priests in the Bible were married.)

AD 1090 – Prayer rosaries started by Peter the hermit, with a pagan Hindu origin.

AD 1190 – Indulgencies – which is time in purgatory supposedly reduced by penance.

AD 1215 – Transubstantiation – the doctrine of the conversion of the Eucharist elements into the actual body and blood of Jesus was also started. (Only the priests were allowed the wine as the laity might spill it.) Confession to receive absolution was also introduced.

AD 1229 – Interpretation of the Bible by the laity was forbidden.

(The above dates can be checked on line.)

In addition, the worship of Mary has been around for a long time as has salvation through infant baptism. It is such a deception to believe one is going to heaven through this.

During this time of the papacy there were faithful believers; for example Francis of Assisi, Madam Guyon and Thomas à Kempis, who wrote 'The Imitation of Christ'.

Jesus' introduction to this church describes Himself as 'the Son of God who has eyes like a flame of fire, and His feet like fine brass' (Revelation 2:18, and see for comparison Daniel 10:6). This is judgment yet to come on the harlotry of Jezebelism, a judgment by the Lord described in Revelation 1:14-15.

All these rules and traditions are present today in the Catholic Church and even in the Church of England some also believe that if they have been baptised as babies, have gone through confirmation, have been married in the Church of England and finally are buried at the church, then they are fit for heaven. The truth is that if they have not been born again with a personal relationship with the Lord Jesus, they will not have eternal life. The true answer, of course, is for the sinner to repent and ask Jesus into their life (see John 3:3, 14-18, 36).

CHAPTER FIFTEEN

The Church of Sardis

The Dead Church of Revelation 3:1-6

The ancient city of Sardis was a natural fortress set on top of rocky cliffs. It had been fabulously wealthy in its early days. By the time John wrote Revelation the city was great only in name, living on its past reputation saying 'You have a name that you are alive, but you are dead' (v.1).

'Sardis', 'sardius', 'sardine' are all names of a red jewel mentioned in both the Old and New Testaments. It seems to have taken its name from words in Hebrew – *'odem'*, Latin – *'carno'*, and Greek – *'sarx'*, all meaning 'flesh'. So the predominant feature of this city and church period was fleshliness, having a form of godliness without the power and given over to formal or ritualistic worship. They are counselled to 'be watchful and strengthen what remains'; 'hold fast' to the truth they have had 'and repent'.

Sardis was the site of the largest of all Greek temples, it being twice the size of the Parthenon, and also the largest Synagogue ruins ever excavated. There must have been a strong Jewish community within the city.

Prophetically Sardis represents the church of the Reformation, from 1517-1700. The condition of affairs in the realm became intolerable and came to a crisis when Martin Luther nailed his '95 Theses' on the church door in Wittenberg, Germany. Martin Luther and a number of other reformers protested against the false teaching, tyranny and claims of the Papal Church. It was more a struggle for political liberty than purely Christian movement and was the start of denominationalism. 1523 was the start of the Baptist church. 1534 was the start of the Church of England. In 1560 Calvin and Knox started Presbyterianism. Other state churches, such as Lutheran, came into being in Germany and Scandinavia, and Calvinism in Switzerland. Many also held to the doctrine of replacement theology at this time, meaning they believed that the Church had replaced the Jews and Israel and all the promises to Israel in the Old Testament now applied to the Church.

The multiplication of sects and denominations brought with it much contention and discord, nor was the Nicolaitan issue dealt with. Many failed to live in the expectation of the coming again of the Lord Jesus. Only a remnant truly followed the Lord. But during this time there was the advantage of encouraging the circulation of the Holy Scriptures as they were translated into English and German; but the people did not know of the baptism in the Holy Spirit. They turned away from idols to God but not 'to wait for His Son from heaven ...' 1 Thessalonians 1: 9-10.

Leaven was present because of the different denominations segregating the Church of Jesus Christ, e.g. Baptists on baptism, Calvinism on predestination, Protestants held to the doctrine of the Nicolaitans and many other traditions. Infant baptism does not secure salvation, nor does confirmation unless the young person is truly born again. My grandfather was put out of the Church of England because he refused to confirm young people unless they were truly born again; but that was in the 1920s.

The Reformation did bring in justification by faith in Christ making us acceptable to God – but good works were looked upon as a product and evidence of their salvation. If the reformers had pooled their revelations of the truths together they could have avoided all this segregation. Jesus desires unity of all believers to worship Him and to love Him and each other. "God is Spirit, and those who worship Him must worship in spirit and in truth" (John 4:24). His desire is that we all should be one (see John 17).

"Remember therefore how you have received and heard; hold fast and repent" the Lord says (Revelation 3:3). Let us therefore repent of our denominational differences and turn to the Holy Scriptures and seek the Lord as the Bereans did in the early church (Acts 17:10-11).

'But you, beloved, building yourselves up on your most holy faith, praying in the Holy Spirit, keep yourselves in the love of God, looking for the mercy of our Lord Jesus Christ unto eternal life' (Jude 20).

CHAPTER SIXTEEN

The Church of Philadelphia

The Faithful Church of Revelation 3:7-13

Philadelphia was founded by Eumenes in 2 BC and named after his loyal brother Attalus. It stood on the edge of very fertile ground and was the wine market of Phrygia, even though the region was prone to earthquakes. Because it was on the main postal route from Rome to the East, it was called 'the Gateway to the East', and was certainly located in a place of great opportunity to witness to passers-by. It was also called 'Little Athens' because of the many temples and many festivals kept by the people there.

Philadelphia means 'love of the brethren'. We are 'taught by God to love one another' (1 Thessalonians 4:9); by God the Father in 1 John 4:7-16; by God the Son, "A new commandment I give to you, that you love one another, as I have loved you ..." (John 13:34); and by God the Holy Spirit '... the love of God has been poured out in our hearts by the Holy Spirit who was given to us' (Romans 5:5). It is the love of God that sends us out to reach the lost in the world. Jesus bid the disciples to go to all nations and preach the gospel, after they were endued with the power of the Holy Spirit (Luke 24:47-49). This church had a vision to reach out to the lost and God 'set before' them 'an open door' and we can this see from its physical situation too (Revelation 3:8).

Jesus presented Himself to this church as 'He who is holy, He who is true' (v.7) – as genuine – for He is 'the Truth' (John 14:6). The martyrs in heaven called the Lord 'holy and true' (Revelation 6:10). Because He is holy He has to judge sin, and because He is true He has to vindicate His people who have been wickedly slain. Jesus has the authority to open and close doors. For instance, 'Shebna' was a wicked leader who God removed from office (see Isaiah 22:15-25). We read 'I will call My servant Eliakim' and 'I will commit Your responsibility into his hand.' 'Eliakim' means 'God will establish', and is a picture of Jesus as a dependable administrator of the affairs of God's people. 'The key of the house of David I will lay on His shoulder ...' (v.22). The one having the key has the authority, and Eliakim was a faithful man and was given the keys of authority. Note that Jesus Christ also has the keys of Hades and of death (Revelation 1:18).

In Acts 14:27 Paul and Barnabas reported to the church at Antioch that God 'had opened the door of faith to the Gentiles'. But in this church in Philadelphia they had two obstacles to overcome, one was their little strength and the other, opposition of the Jews in the city. There is no condemnation of this church; no added leaven.

Prophetically we can see that the Philadelphian church represented the years from AD 1740 – 1900 or thereabouts, with the evangelistic and missionary movements, some of which continue to today; so it was the dead Sardis church revived. In particular, in those years there were George Whitfield, John Wesley, Charles Finney and D.L. Moody.

In 1793 William Carey sailed for India where he found an open door. Since then the doors opened into China, Japan, Korea, Africa and the West Indies.

This Philadelphian church was to be kept 'from the hour of temptation', the Tribulation (Revelation 3.10). In the 1880s Dr. H. Grattan Guinness[1], an eminent astronomer became convinced that God was fulfilling the time prophecy of Daniel 4. On the strength of his findings he confidently pointed ahead to the years 1917, 1923 and 1933 as bound to see movement relating to the restoration of Israel to her land.' See page 13 of 'Miracle of Time' by Frank L. Paine.

[1] 'Light for the Last Days' by Henry Grattan Guinness, 1887

CHAPTER SEVENTEEN

The Church of Laodicea

The Lukewarm Church of Revelation 3:14-22

The city of Laodicea was formerly called Diospolis meaning 'city of God' – once a city, or people of God. It was renamed by King Antiochus II in 2 BC after his wife Laodicea. This name comes from '*laos*' – 'people' and '*dike*' – 'law, manner or custom' meaning 'The will of the people' or 'self-rule.' In John's day it had become a self-governed city. It was a prosperous, commercial meeting place, quite self-sufficient, so much so that after a disastrous earthquake in AD 60 it declined financial aid from Rome.

Laodicea lay at a crossroads and became a centre for banking and trade, manufacturing black woollen goods. It had an important medical school which produced tablets and powders and was famous for its special eye-salve. It was surrounded by fertile land in a river valley, but its water supply came down from hot springs in Hierapolis further up the valley, so that by the time it reached Laodicea the water was lukewarm – 'neither hot nor cold' (v.15) as the Lord says about the church there.

The wealthy, proud Laodiceans were in fact in spiritual poverty. Their faith was as sickening as their water, their garments black not white, and the richly clothed citizens were, in the Lord's eyes, naked. Their eye-salve could not open their eyes to the true righteousness, riches and healing in Jesus. They had become so blind to God that they had shut the door on Him.

All this was true at the time the letter was written. Even more so is it true of the church today.

This is the last of the letters to the seven churches and has a very important message for today especially in the Western world. We cannot afford to ignore God's last words to His Church, as they could prove to be the last warning we receive before God's judgements fall on this world. This could be our last chance of obeying God and avoiding His displeasure. It is the most severe message with no words of praise.

Paul with Timothy wrote the Epistle of Colossians, to the saints and faithful brethren in Colosse, with the request to have it read to the Church in Laodicea because of the great conflict (struggle) which he was having for them (Colossians 2:1). Colosse, Laodicea and Hierapolis were neighbouring towns and are mentioned in Colossians 4:12-15.

We can read the Colossian Epistle as applying to the days we are living in now and compare it with Revelation 3:14-22. To the previous church of Philadelphia which had had great recovery of truth, Jesus had said that they had a little strength and had kept His Word and not denied His name (v.8). The key to strength was faithfulness to the Lord Jesus and obedience to His Word, and He found nothing of which to reprove them. But in Laodicea He had nothing for which to commend them and said "I will spew you out of My mouth" (v.16). Sadly, this is the state of much of the church today in the western world. God knows the urgent need of this truth to reach our hearts and conscience. It is the works and testimonies that the Lord judges because His people are His light-bearers to the world which is heading for judgement. Look what He says in v.20, "I stand at the door and knock, if anyone hears **My** voice and opens the door, I will come into **him**", (**<u>not</u> the Church**), "and dine with **him**, and he with Me". And in v.21 we have the Rapture of the Church, "To him who overcomes I will grant to sit with Me on My throne."

Very sadly today, many churches have become a social gathering, singing modern songs with no deep meaning, there is no study of the Bible and immorality is rife. Also any translation of the Bible will do. The whole church is without power, and is sick. See Genesis 2:24 on marriage. Jesus says in Matthew 21:13, "It is written, My house shall be called a house of prayer but you have made it a den of thieves".

The book of Revelation is prophetic and also a book of judgement. In the seven addresses to the churches in Asia the Lord Jesus is seen in His capacity as the judge of His people's works and says to each church that He knows their works.

Laodicea is the last of Revelation's churches before the Rapture of the Church of Jesus Christ and says, "Anoint your eyes with eye salve that you may see" (Revelation 3:18). The anointing of the Holy Spirit is so that we can see; have our eyes open to truth and error, understanding, enlightenment and revelation.

The record of Lot leaving Sodom is very much a picture of the Church being raptured out of this world before the start of the Tribulation. Look at Genesis 19:1-16. In v.3 they ate unleavened bread – and we know what that represents – feeding on the Word in sincerity and truth. In v6 Lot went out to the evil Sodomites to turn them away, but they were violently against Lot who had sat in the gate - he was the gate keeper; meaning he had tried to be a judge to them. The angels had to rescue Lot from them, and in v.11 the angels smote the men with blindness so that they could not find the door. The next day Lot and his two daughters went out of Sodom away from the destruction of the city.

See Judges 16. The **last** of the Judges was Samson, who can be compared to the Church, and Delilah as a type of the world, who had encircled and destroyed his Naziriteship just like the world has encircled God's people and taken from them their sight. In v.20 it says that Samson knew not that the Lord had departed from him, even as the Lord is saying today, "you do not know" (Revelation 3:17). Samson had his eyes put out and he was bound with bronze fetters. His strength was gone (Judges 16:21).

What happened to the **last** of the Kings of Judah before the remnant of the nation was taken captive to Babylon? See 2 Kings 24:19-20. King Zedekiah 'did evil in the sight of the Lord' and God finally cast out the kings from His presence. In 25:7 'They put out the eyes of Zedekiah and bound him in bronze fetters ...'. Samson and Zedekiah's sight had gone and they were bound with fetters of bronze.

So from these various Scriptural examples we see just how significant are the Lord's final acts and deeds with these people and situations – an important lesson we can apply to the Laodicean church – the **last** of the churches.

This final letter – to Laodicea – has become our own prophetic message, but also, the substances of the last four letters do actually exist until the ascension of the Church. Thyatira is the Papacy, dominating a large part of the earth, and is under that woman Jezebel (Revelation 2:20), so that address would apply in such countries where it dominates; also with Sardis representing the post-Reformation phase of testimony. As we have seen the Lord warns Protestantism that it has a name that it lives but to Him it is dead. He says 'for I have not found your works perfect before God ... repent.' But among them there are some who He commends as 'not having defiled their garments' (Revelation 3:2-4).

There are many also who love and faithfully serve the Lord. The Philadelphia phase represents the great recovery of light and truth around 200 years ago making possible the worldwide spread of the Gospel, when the Spirit of God worked mightily in the hearts of a faithful few and, as a result, all over the earth there are today thousands meeting on Scriptural and Apostolic grounds.

This is a commendation to the church which will endure to the end – the faithful church of Philadelphia. Many are persecuted, meeting in homes in secret. They may only have one Bible between them. The Lord says, "You have a little strength, have kept My word and have not denied My name" (3:8). The key of strength was faithfulness to the Person of Jesus and strict obedience to His word, as was said earlier.

The church of Laodicea was to Jesus in a state of unspeakable repulsion. Mercifully God knows the urgent need of truth to reach our hearts and consciences.

The sin of today's church is laid out in this letter – spiritual poverty, dead faith, uncleanness, selfishness, worldliness, laziness, greed and blindness to the truth of God.

Remember Enoch walked with God. We are empowered to witness by the Holy Spirit with a warning to the unsaved around us, for whom we are responsible.

Remedies

Faith – the lukewarmness is now a present-day reality. Our safety, freedom and material well-being has had the same effect on us as it did on the Laodiceans, who said, 'we have need of nothing'. The Lord offered 'gold refined in the fire' which was to be bought and not taken as an easy free gift. Great effort is required to obtain this true gold and to preserve it through the fire of refining (vv.17-18).

'The genuineness of your faith, being much more precious than gold that perishes, though it is tested by fire, may be found to praise, honour and glory at the revelation of Jesus Christ' (1 Peter 1:7).

We do need to confess our unshakeable faith in the Word of God and to stand on that Word in any circumstance. We also need to be clear about the calling to suffer with Him in the last days – to accept both prosperity and adversity. The Lord's covenant requires us to abandon all our worldly interests - and even life itself, if necessary – to follow Him (see Luke 9:62).

Righteousness – our robe of righteousness is that of the Lord's own sinless purity, which He provided for us at Calvary (Isaiah 61:10). Paul says 'put on the Lord Jesus Christ, and make no provision for the flesh, to fulfil its lusts' (Romans 13:14). 'For as many of you as were baptised into Christ have put on Christ' (Galatians 3:27). God wants us walking in the light as He is in the light of truth, fellowshipping with Him in His Word, trusting Him, obeying Him and praising Him. Do we spend time in His presence alone or, together in families teaching our children daily; bringing them up in the nurture and admonition of the Lord, to know the Scriptures, and to praise Him? Or are we too distracted by business, routine and habit?

I am reminded of a hymn by William Dunn Longstaff (1822-94):

Take time to be Holy! Speak oft with your Lord;
Abide in Him always, and feed on His Word.
Make friends of God's children; help those who are weak;
Forgetting in nothing His blessing to seek.

Discernment – Possibly the most vital requirement for a lukewarm Laodicean Christian of today is the God-given ability to see the Truth – the inward witness. The sad fact is that very many Christians are falling away right now, and don't even know it. They are blind to their error simply because they have forsaken the inward witness of the Spirit, and chosen to listen to men. That discernment is supposed to be active and fresh, not dulled by self-will and self-love. If we follow God alone, intent on seeking Him at every turn, we can't go far wrong. But if we follow self-comfort, enjoyment, excitement, popularity – we quench the voice of the Spirit.

'These things say the Amen, the Faithful and True Witness, the beginning of the Creation of God' (Revelation 3:14).

Now the Lord, down through the past ages, has definitely associated Himself with His people in their testimony on earth. He identified Himself with the Christians at Damascus, e.g. Ananias, who prayed for Saul to receive His sight. He was identified with the Reformers such as Luther and others; at other times with the Quakers or Wesley and Whitfield and those with them. Later, He definitely identified Himself with the recovery of Light which brought the Brethren movement into existence, which soon left out the works as James says, 'faith without works is dead'. So then the Lord identified Himself with the Salvation Army who took notice of the needs of the poor. Next was the Convention Movement teaching practical holiness as with believers to walk in victory over sin, by union with the risen Christ.

We do wish, however, that present-day teachers were more consciously aware of the present hour and of the nearness of the Lord's coming; so that their messages might better meet the needs of God's people. But sadly most of the theological colleges omit the teaching of truth concerning the importance of Israel today, and much is centred on the traditions and teachings of man, meaning that their church leaders are in deception themselves.

'As many as I love, I rebuke and chasten. Therefore be zealous and repent.' This is addressed to us by the Lord

(Revelation 3:19). This command of Christ's is His last pre-translation Word to His people on earth. Jesus says that He hoped they would be either cold or hot because if one is only warm it means that there had been a zeal for Him which has dwindled. Can He allow Satan and the world to look on, while His name is linked with the evils of His people with whom He has publicly associated Himself?

Jesus is coming to judge the world in righteousness.

'He who has an ear, let him hear what the Spirit says to the churches' (v.22).

Note

In the next chapter, which I have called 'Admonitions', there are Scriptures to help us to know what we can do to prepare us for Jesus to return as our Bridegroom.

CHAPTER EIGHTEEN

Admonitions

We have established that we are very close to the return of Christ to reign over this earth for a thousand years (Revelation 20:1-6). And we know from Scripture that there will be a seven-year period called 'the Tribulation' beforehand, when God will deal with His Jewish people whilst judging this world, Revelation chapters 6-16. During that time the enemy, Satan, will be trying to take over this world and to set up a kingdom from Jerusalem.

Therefore what sort of people ought we to be and what encouragement can we glean from the Scriptures, to prepare for the Rapture of His Bride by Jesus before the Tribulation begins?

I want to encourage us to draw nearer to God than we ever have before and to spend time in His presence in the Word.

1 Thessalonians 1:10 literally says, 'We are to wait for God's Son from heaven, whom He raised from the dead, even Jesus, who is delivering us from the wrath to come'. (Hebrew: The word 'delivering' is in the present continuous tense; in other words it is living, happening now and continuing to happen).

'Knowing the time that now it is high time to awake out of sleep; for now is our salvation nearer than when we believed. The day is at hand; let us put on the armour of light ... put on the Lord Jesus Christ, and make no provision for the flesh ...' (Romans 13:11-14).

'Therefore my beloved brethren, be steadfast, immoveable, always abounding in the work of the Lord ...' (1 Corinthians 15:58).

'For our conversation is in heaven; from whence also we look for the Saviour, the Lord Jesus Christ' (Philippians 3:20, KJV).

'Beware lest any man spoil you through philosophy and vain deceit, after the tradition of men, after the rudiments of the world, and not after Christ' (Colossians 2:8, KJV).

'Set your mind', or affections, 'on things above, not on things on the earth'. 'Let the word of Christ dwell in you richly in all wisdom, teaching and admonishing one another ...' and 'Whatever you do in word or deed, do all in the name of the Lord Jesus, giving thanks to God the Father through Him' (Colossians 3:2, 16-17).

The Thessalonian Epistles are the only books that do not refer back to the Old Testament. 'May the Lord make you increase and abound in love one toward another'... 'so that He may establish your hearts blameless in holiness before our God and Father at the coming of our Lord Jesus Christ with all His saints' (1 Thessalonians 3:12-13).

'For this is the will of God, your sanctification' ... (1 Thessalonians 4:3). For God has called us ... 'unto holiness' (v.7 KJV). '... God, who has also given us His Holy Spirit' (v.8). Also see Titus 2:11-14.

'The God of peace sanctify you completely; and may your whole spirit and soul and body be preserved blameless at the coming of our Lord Jesus Christ. He who calls you is faithful, who also will do it' (1 Thessalonians 5:23-24).

'But you, beloved, building yourselves up on your most holy faith, praying in the Holy Spirit, keep yourselves in the love of God, looking for the mercy of our Lord Jesus Christ unto eternal life. And on some have compassion, making a distinction; but others save with fear, pulling them out of the fire, hating even the garment defiled by the flesh. Now to Him who is able to keep you from stumbling, and to present you faultless before the presence of His glory with exceeding joy, to God our Saviour, who alone is wise, be glory and majesty, dominion and power, both now and forever. Amen' (Jude 20-25).

'For if you live according to the flesh you shall die; but if by the Spirit you put to death the deeds of the body, you shall live' (Romans 8:13).

'... Work out your own salvation with fear and trembling; for it is God who works in you both to will and to do for His good pleasure' (Philippians 2:12b-13).

Prayer

'Where two or three are gathered together in My name there am I in the midst of them' (Matthew 18:20).

'Your Will be done on earth as it is in heaven, and forgive us our sins, as we also forgive everyone who is indebted to us' (Luke 11:2 and 4).

'Praying always with all prayer and supplication in the Spirit, being watchful to this end ... for all the saints' (Ephesians 6:18).

Pray for your nation using Daniel 9:4-19. Pray for God to forgive us for being so divided by denominational barriers and that Jesus' prayer of John 17 will be answered. Jesus prayed, "for those who will believe in Me through their word; that they all may be one, as You, Father, are in Me, and I in You; that they also may be one in Us, that the world may believe that You sent Me. And the glory which You gave Me I have given them, that they may be one just as We are one: I in them, and You in Me, that they may be made perfect in one, and that the world may know that You have sent Me, and have loved them as You have loved Me"(John 17:20-23).

Pray for Israel, 'Pray for the peace of Jerusalem: May they prosper who love you' (Psalm 122:6). There is so much misunderstanding concerning the Land of Israel and of the Jews by the Church today. One thought is that God has finished with Israel as a nation. Briefly:- The Land of Israel is God's and He gave it to Israel for an everlasting possession '... and all this land that I have spoken of I give to your descendants, and they shall inherit it forever' (Exodus 32:13b). People in the Book of Genesis were all Gentile, but God chose out a people for Himself through Abraham, Isaac and Jacob, who was later called Israel. God gave them the land of Canaan as an everlasting possession. He called it His Land, and they are His people and the city of Jerusalem is His city. Jesus came through the tribe of Judah. His mother was descended from King David through Solomon and his son, Nathan.

All this you know. The Romans destroyed the Temple and Jerusalem in AD 70 and the Jews were dispersed (called the Diaspora) throughout the world for a set time as given in the book of Daniel. God has brought them back, (called the Aaliyah), to their land on time in God's timetable, and the nation was reborn in a day in 1948. God has been establishing them there in the Promised Land of Israel in spite of the world's antagonism, and rejection by the established churches.

Romans 9-11 are very enlightening to read. We need to recognise that God has a purpose for His original covenant people and through the Tribulation to come, they will finally see that Jesus is their Messiah and King (11:26). Looking at Matthew 24 Jesus is asked by his disciples about when these things will come to pass. He says "Now learn this parable from the fig tree": (referring to the nation of Israel) "When its branch has already become tender and puts forth leaves, you know that summer is near. So you also, when you see all these things, know that it is near, at the very doors. ... this generation" – (the generation alive in 1948) "will by no means pass away till all these things are fulfilled. ..."My words will by no means pass away" (vv.32-35). 'Generation' explained in Psalm 90: 10. 'The days of our lives are seventy years; and if by reason of strength they are eighty years ... it is soon cut off, and we fly away'. Jesus shall return to this earth to set up His Kingdom from Jerusalem. All this is explained in my father's book, 'Miracle of Time' by Frank L. Paine.

One encouraging thought I should like to share with you comes to mind. Do you remember the first 'Sign Miracle' in John 2? It was at a Jewish wedding which lasted seven days and they had run out of wine. The huge, stone water jars were filled to the brim with water and Jesus turned the water into wine. The master of the feast said, "Every man at the beginning sets out the good wine ... but you have kept the good wine until now". 'Jesus manifested His glory; and His disciples believed in Him' (vv.10-11).

Can we believe for God the Father to pour out an abundance of His "good wine" – His Holy Spirit – upon us before He bids His Son our Lord Jesus Christ to come?

CHAPTER NINETEEN

The Feast of Weeks *(Part 2)*

The Ascension of The Church, The Bride of Christ

Nowhere in the Old Testament is there a mention of the Church or Bride of Christ, but, there are pictures or types of her. One beautiful picture is in Genesis 24 where Abraham, the father, sent his servant to fetch a bride, Rebekah, for his son Isaac; likened to God the Father sending the Holy Spirit to seek out a Bride for His Son Jesus.

The Ascension of The Church, The Bride of Christ

Who is the Church, the Bride of Christ? As we explained in my Chapter 10, she comprises all who have believed on the Lord Jesus since His death and resurrection, from every nation and language on earth. Paul says in Ephesians 5:25-27 'Christ also loved the church and gave Himself for it'; 'that He might present it to Himself a glorious church, not having spot, or wrinkle or any such thing ... holy and without blemish'; 'For we are members of His body' (v.30). 'This is a great mystery; but I speak concerning Christ and the church' (v.32).

Jesus says, in John 14:1-3, "Let not your heart be troubled; you believe in God, believe also in Me. In My Father's house are many mansions; if it were not so, I would have told you. I go to prepare a place for you. And if I go and prepare a place for you, I will come again and receive you to Myself; that where I am, there you may be also." Jesus was speaking to His eleven disciples, after Judas Iscariot had left the supper they had together the night Jesus was arrested.

This passage speaks of an event yet future, which we call the 'rapture'. The word 'rapture' is not found in the Bible but is often used by believers to describe the event revealed to us in 1 Corinthians 15:45-54 and in 1 Thessalonians 4:13-18; two passages worth reading again now. 'Rapture' comes from the Latin *'rapio'* meaning 'to carry away, to be caught up, to be raised up'. The word used in the original Greek text is *'harpazo',* which likewise means 'to catch away, take by force'; that is a strong rapid motion, i.e. against gravity – as already explained in my Introduction.

Let us first consider 1 Corinthians 15, where in verses 20-23 we see that the Church, which is His body, has to go through a change to be admitted into heaven. 'For as in Adam all die' so, through believing in Christ and His sacrifice, 'all shall be made alive'. The order is this – 'Christ the firstfruits of those who had fallen asleep during His lifetime and were raised from the dead on the day Jesus rose from the dead (Matthew 27:52-53). Next, it will be 'those who are Christ's at His coming', when all believers from His resurrection to the present day will arise, including the Apostles. Now, look at 1 Corinthians 15:42-57 concerning the resurrection of the dead. 'The body is sown in corruption; it is raised in incorruption'.... 'It is sown in weakness, it is raised in power'. 'It is sown a natural body, it is raised a spiritual body'... 'And so it is written, "The first man Adam became a living being." The last Adam became a life-giving spirit. ... The second Man is the Lord from heaven' (v.47). The first is 'natural and afterwards the spiritual' (v. 46). Those born of the Spirit shall be raised to life eternal for 'as we have borne the image of the man of dust, we shall also bear the image of the heavenly Man' (v.49), and 'flesh and blood cannot inherit the kingdom of God; nor does corruption inherit incorruption' (v.50).

Now, what about all those who are alive when Jesus comes for His Bride? This is the mystery of the final harvest. 'We shall not all sleep, but we shall all be changed – 'at the last trumpet. For the trumpet will sound, and the dead will be raised incorruptible.' But for the living, 'we shall be changed; for this corruptible must put on incorruption, and this mortal must put on immortality ... then shall be brought to pass the saying that is written: "Death is swallowed up in victory"' (vv.51-54).

Turning now to 1 Thessalonians 4:13-18 we are able to see the order of events at the Rapture[1]. We can measure the importance of these events because Paul tells us that he does not want us to be ignorant of them (v.13). He continues, 'if we believe that Jesus died and rose again, even so God will bring with Him (Jesus) those who sleep in Jesus' (v.14). 'For the Lord Himself will descend from heaven with a shout, with the voice of an archangel, and with the trumpet of God' (sounded from heaven). 'And the dead in Christ will rise first.' 'Then' (correct translation is 'Afterwards') having been changed in the twinkling of an eye at the last trumpet (1 Corinthians 15:51-52), we who are alive and remain 'shall be caught up together with them in the clouds to meet the Lord in the air. And thus we shall always be with the Lord' (1 Thessalonians 4:16-17).

It is no problem to God to raise the dead, since He made Adam from the dust of the earth. Ecclesiastes 12:7 says 'Then the dust will return to the earth as it was, and the spirit will return to God who gave it' – showing what happens to everyone who dies. At the first trumpet the dead shall be raised from land and sea. Afterwards 'we who are alive and remain' shall be changed, as the last trumpet summons all the Bride of Christ to be 'caught up together', 'in the clouds to meet the Lord in the air. And so we shall always be with the Lord. Therefore comfort one another with these words' (1 Thessalonians 4:17-18).

You will have noticed that there are two trumpets, the 'first' and the 'last'. We shall look at these more specifically later, but it is worth noting that there are over 100 references to trumpets in the Bible. Some refer to the 'shofar' – the ram's horn, and some to the silver trumpets of Numbers 10:1-10. This precious metal – silver – speaks to us of redemption. This is best seen in the price paid for the betrayal of Christ who was our ransom (see Zechariah 11:12-13 and Matthew 26:15). Numbers 10:2 says 'you may use them (the trumpets) for the call of the assembly, and the journeying of the camps. When they shall blow with them, all the assembly shall assemble themselves to you at the door of the Tabernacle of the congregation.' Similarly, Psalm 47:5 says 'God has gone up with a shout, the Lord with the sound of a trumpet.' So, we see that trumpets have much to do with calling the people to order, and movement in some shape or form. No wonder that the rapture involves trumpets, and indeed, trumpets sounded from heaven!

Jesus will Return and Fulfill the Feast of Weeks

Earlier, we saw that Jesus only fulfilled 40 days of the Feast of Weeks to Pentecost, the feast of harvest, leaving 9 days still unfulfilled when there was neither Jesus the Son of God, nor the Holy Spirit on the earth[1]. This is significant because Jesus said that He had come to fulfil the law (Matthew 5:17-18). Romans 10:4 confirms this, 'For Christ is the end of the law ...'. The Greek word used here for 'end' is '*telos*' which means 'aim, completion, purpose, goal, outcome or consummation'.

In Leviticus 23:15-17 we read 'you shall count for yourselves from the day after the Sabbath' (remember the morning of Jesus' resurrection), 'from the day that you brought the sheaf of the wave offering: seven Sabbaths shall be completed. Count fifty days to the day after the seventh Sabbath; then you shall offer a new grain offering to the Lord. You shall bring from your dwellings two wave loaves of two-tenths of an ephah. They shall be of fine flour; they shall be baked with leaven. They are the firstfruits to the Lord.' It continues in verse 20, 'The priest shall wave them with the bread of the firstfruits as a wave offering before the Lord.' How wonderful! The Harvest of the firstfruits brought in.

At Pentecost, the 50th day after Jesus' resurrection, the Holy Spirit came on the Church – see Acts 2 – ushering in the Church Age of these nearly 2,000 years. Could it be that these nine days will take place between the dead rising to life at Jesus' descent and His ascension with His Bride, between the two trumpet blasts. We see in Matthew 27:52-53 that when Jesus rose from the dead the graves were opened and many bodies of the **saints** were raised and appeared to many. This will be the whole harvest brought in? Jesus will be here on earth during these nine days appearing to his Bride around the earth? See again Leviticus 23:15, '... seven Sabbaths shall be **completed**'.

Now, we ought to consider the two wave loaves of Leviticus 23:17 and 20 mentioned above. 'You shall bring from your dwellings two wave loaves of two-tenths of an ephah. They shall be of fine flour; they shall be baked with leaven. They are the firstfruits to the LORD ... The priest shall wave them with the bread of the firstfruits as a wave offering before the LORD.' We see these two loaves as Jew and Gentile, while the fine flour, as we have previously seen, speaks of the pure truth of Jesus, but baked with leaven, as the church has become leavened down this Age. Leaven is the corruption of the Word of God by man's interpretation so the church has become leavened by the traditions and denominational differences now ingrained in her (see Jesus' parable in Matthew 13:33 and Luke 13:20-21) which we have mentioned earlier in Chapter 11 – 'How Leaven Has Entered The Church of Jesus Christ'.

All down the 2,000 years since Jesus made the promise, "if I go away I will come again and receive you to **Myself**" (John 14:3), the church of Jesus Christ has lived her life in anticipation of His imminent return. Such anticipation has kept true believers living upright lives, 'looking unto Jesus the author and finisher of their faith' (Hebrews 12:2). So, how is it that many Christians in this 21st Century now consider that the Rapture will take place either halfway through the Tribulation or at the end of it, meaning that they are not believing in the imminence of Jesus' return? It seems the devil is busy deceiving the Bride of Christ as to this vital matter.

The Tribulation to come, as described in the book of Revelation chapters 6-16, has a definite start date, when a covenant is confirmed with (Hebrew is *'forced upon'*) Israel by the Antichrist (Daniel 9:27) for one week (Hebrew: *'Sheva'* meaning seven) of years. Jesus said, "I have come in My Father's name, and you do not receive Me; if another comes in his own name, him you will receive" (John 5:43, see also Isaiah 28:14-15). The seven-year Tribulation is measured in 360-day (Babylonian) years; as explained at the end of my Chapter 4.

As we look around us, one thing is certain; the world is getting close to those days. Romans 1:18-32, 2 Peter 2 and Luke 21:7-11 all give further detail for comparison with today. Jesus, when instructing His disciples regarding the signs, says in Luke 21:28, "Now when these things begin to happen, look up and lift up your heads, because your redemption draws near." The greatest sign for the imminence of the Rapture of the Church is that the Jews are back in their own land fulfilling many prophecies; such as Isaiah 66:8-10 and Jeremiah 31:8-10, 27-28.

It appears to me that Paul, when writing 1 Thessalonians under the auspices of the Holy Spirit, was looking forward to the days we are living in now, in this 21st Century. There are some interesting verses ending each chapter of this Epistle: 'wait for His Son from heaven ... even Jesus who delivers us from the wrath to come' (1:10); 'we shall be in the presence of our Lord Jesus Christ at His coming' (2:19), 'so that He may establish your hearts blameless in holiness before our God and Father at the coming of our Lord Jesus Christ with all His saints' (3:13); 'God has not appoint us to wrath, but to obtain salvation through our Lord Jesus Christ' (5:9-10). May I suggest you read the whole of 1 Thessalonians with this in mind?

Revelation Chapters 4 and 5

The Book of Revelation is written in chronological order. Chapter 4 begins, 'After these things...', that is, after chapters 2 and 3, which are literal and prophetic about the seven churches through the Church Age. Revelation 4:1-4 also reveals the time of Harvest; John is shown a **door** open in heaven and a voice as it were of a trumpet saying "come up here." We can compare this with 1 Corinthians 15:52, where the Church will be caught up to meet the Lord in the air 'at the last trumpet'.

Continuing in Revelation 4:3-4, we are told that John sees in heaven a throne and 'round the throne are twenty-four seats and on the seats twenty-four elders clothed in white raiment.' Why twenty-four? 24 is the number connected with the priesthood (see 1 Chronicles 24:7–19) which sets out the number of priestly courses for the Temple. These were formed on the "pattern of things in the heavens." They were the leaders of the heavenly worship, according to Bullinger[2]. There are seven references to these elders in the Book of Revelation and they are always seen in heaven. They are arrayed in white raiment which speaks of righteousness (provided by the blood of Jesus) as in

Revelation 5:9-10, 'and they *(the elders)* sang a new song, saying:

"You are worthy to take the scroll,
And to open its seals;
For You were slain,
And have redeemed us to God by Your blood
Out of every tribe and tongue and people and nation,
And have made us kings and priests to our God;
And we shall reign on the earth."'

If we compare Revelation 1:4 'John to the seven churches' with the last chapter, Revelation 22:16 '"I, Jesus, have sent My angel to testify to you these things in the churches', we can see the constant theme of a message to the churches through the ages. Revelation 22:17 continues, 'And the Spirit and the Bride say, "Come!"' So, I believe the Scriptures are clear that the Church is to be taken before the Tribulation begins. After all, the Church worldwide is already suffering greatly in many countries and God wants to deliver her out from the wrath still to come.

Jesus says "Surely I am coming quickly." Amen. Even so, come, LORD JESUS! (Revelation 22:20).

[1] See 'Ten Days At The Rapture' by Brian Gemmell

[2] 'Number in Scripture' by E.W. Bullinger – page 264

CHAPTER TWENTY

The Feasts of the 7th Month

'And He has on His robe and on his thigh a name written KING OF KINGS AND LORD OF LORDS.'
Revelation 19:16

The three feasts of the seventh month, Feast of Trumpets, Day of Atonement and Feast of Tabernacles are described in Leviticus 23:23-43.

After much searching I believe that these feasts are to do with the Jewish people at the beginning of the Millennium, the seventh thousand years; the reign of the Messiah on the earth as King of Kings and Lord of Lords. This will be at the end of the seven years of Tribulation. By then the Jews will know that Jesus was and is their Messiah as the veil is taken away from their hearts (see Romans 11:25-27 and 2 Corinthians 3:15-16).

Why at the start of the Millennium? As I pondered upon these feasts, I was reminded that the **seventh** day of every week is a Sabbath (see Genesis 2:1-4). God blessed the **seventh** day and v.4 says 'this is the **history** (Hebrew: '*toledoth*', meaning 'generations', 'genealogies', therefore by implication history') of the heavens and the earth when they were created ...' God rested on the **seventh** day. Since then every Sabbath has looked forward to that seventh thousand years when Jesus shall reign over the whole earth, the devil will be chained up and there will be peace on earth. So why should not these feasts in the **seventh** month look forward to their fulfilment by the Lord Jesus in the Kingdom to come?

Let us look further at these three feasts: the Feast of Trumpets, the Day of Atonement and the Feast of Tabernacles. They were all special Sabbaths on whichever day of the week they occurred (Leviticus 23:24, 32 & 39).

The Feast of Trumpets

Leviticus 23:24-25

Trumpets have been mentioned previously in this book. We have seen that this Feast will not be fulfilled by the Lord Jesus at the Rapture of the Church, as those trumpets will be sounded from heaven. The trumpet sounded on Mount Sinai in Exodus 19 and 20 was also sounded from heaven. Trumpets were sounded in war, as at the fall of Jericho in Joshua 6; Gideon against the Midianites in Judges 7 and by angels in the trumpet Judgments to come in Revelation 8 and 9. Other great occasions when trumpets were sounded were at the laying of the foundation of the second Temple in Ezra 3:10 and at the dedication of the walls of Jerusalem in Nehemiah 12:31-43. Trumpets are blown on the first day of each month at the new moon, but also on the Feast of Trumpets on the first day of the seventh month each year.

So clearly trumpets have a central place in God's dealings with His covenant people, all the more so when Jesus Himself fulfils the Feast of Trumpets. Trumpets were blown at the celebrations for the crowning of kings, as of King Solomon in 1 Kings 1:39 and 41; also of King Joash in 2 Chronicles 23:11-13. The greatest sounding of trumpets recorded in the Bible is at the dedication of Solomon's Temple in 2 Chronicles 5:11-14 'the Levites who were the singers ... clothed in white linen', having instruments, 'and with them 120 priests sounding with trumpets' ... that 'when the trumpeters and singers were as one, to make one sound to be heard in praising and thanking the LORD ... that the house of the LORD, was filled with a cloud, so that the priests could not continue ministering ... for the glory of the LORD, filled the house of God'. In a parallel passage in 1 Kings 8:2 it says this was at the feast of the seventh month on Mount Zion.

When Jesus comes to reign as King of kings on Mount Zion and Ezekiel's Temple is dedicated, surely there will be a tremendous celebration and dedication. May be Psalms 47 and 98 will be used for praise and worship at that time!

The Day of Atonement

Leviticus 23:27-32

This day was to be kept on the 10th day of the 7th month. This is the Most Holy Day in the Jewish calendar. It is a convocation (Sabbath) on which ever day of the week it falls; a day to afflict the soul, humbling of self, atoning for sin and rest from labour. A full description of it is given in Leviticus 16 as to how Israel was to keep it. The offerings there looked forward to one day when One, the Holy Son of Man, represented by the animals offered, would shed His sinless blood, dying outside the city with malefactors to take away our sin, to cleanse us from all wrong and to clothe us in robes of righteousness. It is because of this all-encompassing sacrifice of the Lord Jesus that God can have any dealings with this fallen world, with such love and compassion, grace and patience. Hebrews 2:9 says 'He, by the grace of God, might taste death for everyone'.

2 Corinthians 5:21 reminds us that God 'made Him who knew no sin to be sin for us ... 'Atonement means 'covering'. The Hebrew is *'kaphar'* which is a primary root meaning – to cover, to expiate, to cancel, appease, to make an atonement = cleanse, pardon, purge (away). The Greek word is *'hiliasmos'* = 'propitiate' (1 John 2:2 and 4:10). There is so much more to this feast which we do not have room for here, but, we can look at:

God's Hidden Day of Atonement in the Life and Death of Jesus

John 12:1-35

In the calendar of the days of the Lord's own life, 27th April AD 33 (the Jews' 10th Nisan) at 6pm was the Day of Atonement in Jesus' 34th year; this was when Mary of Bethany anointed Jesus for burial. Here Jesus is seen presenting Himself before God as the antitype of the offerings of the Day of Atonement. Matthew 26:12 "For in pouring this fragrant oil on My body, she did it for My burial" (embalming). In John 12:7 Jesus says "Let her alone; she has kept this for the day of My burial". Jesus is therefore represented as dying (as in a picture). Affliction of the soul is seen in Leviticus 16:29 and Isaiah 53:4 and 7. To afflict in Hebrew is *'anah'* = 'afflict lower'. This has the idea of looking down; abasing self, chasten self, humbling oneself (Strong's Concordance). Read John 12:23-33 where in verse 27 Jesus said, "Now My soul is troubled (or afflicted) and what shall I say? 'Father, save Me from this hour'? But for this purpose I came to this hour. Father, glorify your name". He was magnifying the law by afflicting His soul on this hidden Day of Atonement.

[The Yom Kippur war started on 6th October 1973 at 2pm, when Syria and Egypt attacked Israel on Israel's Day of Atonement. This was 2,000 lunar years from 27th April AD 33 – God's Hidden Day of Atonement. See 'Miracle of Time' page 99[1].]

At the start of the Kingdom when Yeshua HaMashiach – Jesus the Messiah – comes to reign, the Day of Atonement will be fulfilled. Revelation 1:7 says 'Behold, He is coming with clouds, and every eye will see Him, and they also who pierced Him. And all the tribes of the earth will mourn because of Him'. Read Zechariah 12:10-14 '... then they will look on Me whom they have pierced; they will mourn for Him as one mourns for his only son, and grieve for Him as one grieves for a firstborn. In that day there shall be a great mourning in Jerusalem' (vv.10-11; also see Matthew 24:30-31). 'In that day a fountain shall be opened for the house of David and for the inhabitants of Jerusalem, for sin and for uncleanness' (Zechariah 13:1). Israel and Judah will come together weeping to seek the LORD their God and to join themselves to the Lord 'in a perpetual covenant that will not be forgotten' (Jeremiah 50:5).

The Feast of Tabernacles

Leviticus 23:33-36, 39-43

This feast is kept on 15th of the seventh month for seven days with an eighth day. The first and eighth days are 'Holy Convocations'. This was a compulsory feast for the men of Israel to attend yearly in Jerusalem. It is also called the Feast of Ingathering, the harvest of olives – oil, and grapes – wine. Oil is the symbol of the Holy Spirit's anointing, and wine is a symbol of joy and blessing (see Psalm 104:15).

The Lord instructs Ezekiel to keep the feasts in the Millennium (Ezekiel 45:18-25). 'In the seventh month, on the fifteenth day of the month, at the feast', the Feast of Tabernacles, they were to offer sin offerings, a burnt offering to the LORD and grain offerings and oil for seven days.

The Eighth Day: can you see an eighth day depicting the Eternal Order to follow the 7,000 years? This feast is to be kept with great joy and great gladness. In the Millennium the nations will 'go up from year to year to worship the King, the LORD of hosts, and keep the Feast of Tabernacles' (Zechariah 14:16-21). Jesus, at the Feast of Tabernacles, is found in John 7:2, 37-39, 'Now the Jews' Feast of Tabernacles was at hand' ... 'on that last day, that great day of the feast, Jesus stood and cried out saying, "If any one thirsts, let him come unto Me and drink, he who believes in Me, as the Scripture has said, out of his heart will flow rivers of living water." But this He spoke concerning the Spirit, whom those believing in Him would receive.' Wonderful words! Here are some great Psalms of praise, Psalm 67, Psalm 86:9-12, Psalm 89:1-18, and Psalm 72:19 says, 'Blessed be His glorious name forever! And let the whole earth be filled with His glory. Amen.' What a further prospect! – prompting even louder 'Hallelujahs!'

We can't finish here without mentioning the Birth of the Lord Jesus being on the first day of the Feast of Tabernacles in 1 B.C. He was born in the city of David, Bethlehem, meaning 'the House of Bread'. He was laid in a manger – the feeding trough for the sheep – He is the Bread of Life. And He 'became flesh and **dwelt** among us', Greek: *'skenoo'*, to pitch a tent, to tabernacle (John 1:14).

Both Mary and Joseph came from King David's line. Matthew 1:1 says 'Jesus Christ, the son of David' ... King David begat Solomon, whose mother was Bathsheba. All the royal generations of the tribe of Judah came down to Jacob, the father of Joseph, the husband of Mary (v16). In Luke 3:23 Jesus (as was supposed) the son of Joseph, which was the son of Heli; Heli was the father of Mary and her descendants went back to Nathan the son of King David. Bathsheba had five sons by David, and Solomon and Nathan were brothers (see 1 Chronicles 3:5). Peter, on the day of Pentecost, speaks beautifully of David prophesying that of the fruit of his body he would raise up the Christ to sit on his throne (Acts 2:29-36).

[1] 'Miracle of Time' by Frank L. Paine – page 99

AFTERWORD

I hope, as you come to the end of this book that your hunger for God has grown to study the Scriptures for yourselves and desire the deeper truths. There is so much hidden treasure in God's Holy Book. He wants to feed us on 'the finest of the wheat' (Psalm 81:16).

There has been here much to digest and for some it may have been a challenge to what you have heard or believed through previous teachers, TV or books.

We are surely living in turbulent days, perplexity among the nations, rumours of wars, pandemics and violence on our streets all pointing to the end of days as we have known them.

I have prayed much over each chapter to share what the Lord would have me say, barely skimming the surface of these Feasts, their purpose and meanings.

Comparing Scripture with Scripture I do believe will help you to understand God's order of events shortly to take place when Jesus will return as He promised.

It is high time to prepare ourselves to meet our Bridegroom, living a holy life, pleasing God, not ourselves, full of love for Him and each other and the Jews. Let us trim our lamps, be filled with the Holy Spirit, boldly proclaiming the Lord Jesus, the Saviour of the world, to rescue the perishing whilst there is a little time left.

The words of Revelation 22:20 *(KJV)*, 'Surely I come quickly. Amen. Even so, come, Lord Jesus.'

APPENDIX 1

The Feasts of the Lord

Leviticus 23

FEASTS OF
1st MONTH, ABIB (NISAN)

Feeding upon the Truth of God (Jesus)

FEASTS OF
7th MONTH, TISHRI

Abiding in Christ

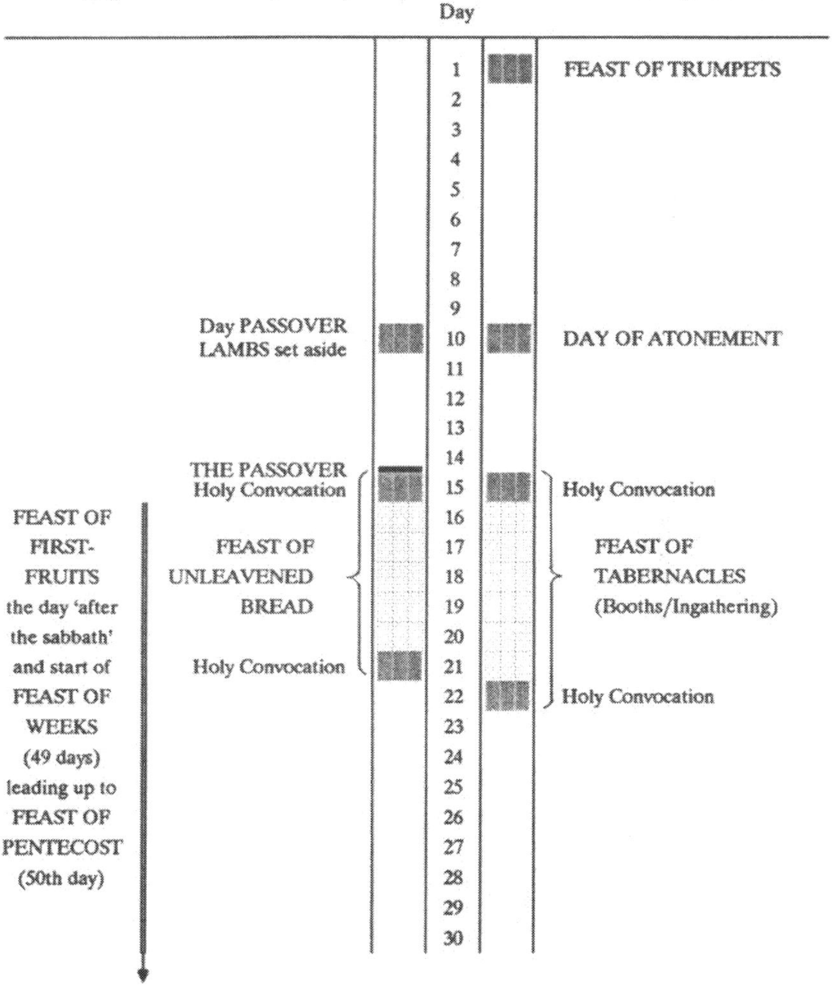

From 'Miracle of Time' page 191

APPENDIX 2

The Seven Days of Unleavened Bread

following the Passover in Egypt in 1639 BC

	Gentile Calendar	Jewish Calendar		
6pm			RAMESES	
	May 11	Abib 14 Nisan		
6pm 12mid			Passover / Unleavened Bread Midnight - death of the firstborn	
	12	15	The Exodus	
6pm			SUCCOTH	
	13	16		3½ days
6pm			ETHAM	
	14	17		
6pm			MIGDOL (Pi-Hahiroth)	
	15	18	Red Sea Crossing Song of Moses	
6pm				
	16	19	Three days in the wilderness Exodus 8: 27	
6pm				3½ days
	17	20		
6pm			MARAH - Exodus 15: 22-27	
	18	21		
6pm			ELIM	

From 'Miracle of Time' page 195

APPENDIX 3

The Fulfilment of The Feast of Weeks

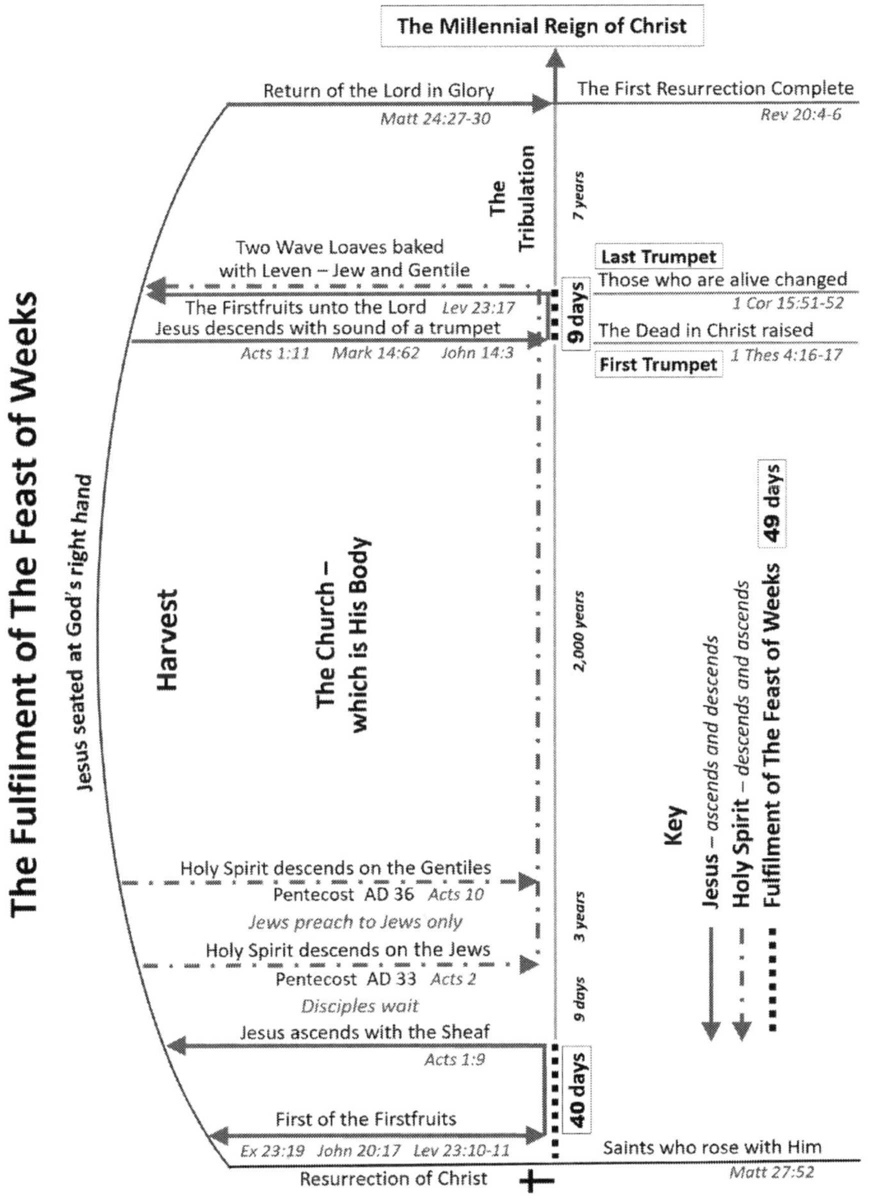

POSTSCRIPT

The Word 'Church'

I have used the word 'church' throughout this book as it is the common word used for and by most denominations, but in the days of Constantine he wanted to unite believers in Jesus with pagans into a named building by using just one word.

The Greek New Testament uses the word *'ekklesia'*. This actually means 'called-out ones'.

Without going into great detail about this issue here there is obviously now confusion as to whether the **people** or a **building** is meant when the word 'church' is used.

To study this further I recommend that you read an article by Andy Zoppelt about this, which is available from:

andyzoppelt.blogspot.com/2021/08/origin-of-word-church-and-its.html

A printable version for private study is available from my webpage:
www.shiloah.co.uk/other-studies1 *under the heading:*
4c) THE LIFE OF JESUS IN RELATION TO TIME – Supplementary material

Miracle of Time

I have referred to my father, Frank Paine's, book many times. There are a few printed copies still available but you may also download a free pdf copy. You will find links to both on my webpage:

www.shiloah.co.uk/miracle-of-time

INDEX

1 241111

Printed in Great Britain
by Amazon

51004836R00075